CAREER IDEAS for teens in

business, management, & administration

The Career Ideas for Teens Series

CAREER IDEAS for teens in

business, management, & administration

Diane Lindsey Reeves,
Joe Rhatigan, and Kelly Gunzenhauser

Ferguson's

An Infobase Learning Company

Career Ideas for Teens in Business, Management, and Administration

Ferguson's
An imprint of Infobase Learning
132 West 31st Street
New York NY 10001

Library of Congress Cataloging-in-Publication Data
Reeves, Diane Lindsey, 1959–
  Career ideas for teens in business, management, and administration / Diane Lindsey Reeves, Joe Rhatigan, and Kelly Gunzenhauser.
       p. cm.
    Includes bibliographical references and index.
    ISBN-13: 978-0-8160-8265-0 (hardcover : alk. paper)
    ISBN-10: 0-8160-8265-0 (hardcover : alk. paper) 1. Business—Vocational guidance.
  2. Management—Vocational guidance. I. Rhatigan, Joe. II. Gunzenhauser, Kelly. III. Title.
    HF5381.R365 2012
    331.7020835—dc22   2011013355

Ferguson's books are available at special discounts when purchased in bulk quantities for businesses, associations, institutions, or sales promotions. Please call our Special Sales Department in New York at (212) 967-8800 or (800) 322-8755.

You can find Ferguson's on the World Wide Web at http://www.infobaselearning.com

Text design and composition by Annie O'Donnell
Cover design by Takeshi Takahashi
Illustrations by Matt Wood
Cover printed by Bang Printing, Brainerd, Minn.
Book printed and bound by Bang Printing, Brainerd, Minn.
Date printed: November 2011

Printed in the United States of America

10 9 8 7 6 5 4 3 2 1

This book is printed on acid-free paper.

CONTENTS

Welcome to Your Future

Q: What is one of the most dreaded questions of the high school experience?

A: What are you going to do after you graduate?

Talk about pressure! You have to come up with an answer sometime soon. But, homecoming is right around the corner; coach called an extra practice; homework is piling up....

Feel free to delay the inevitable. But here's the deal: Sooner or later the same people who make you go to school now are eventually going to make you stop. If you get it right, you'll exit with diploma in hand and at least a general idea of what to do next.

So...

What *are* you going to do after you graduate?

There are plenty of choices. You could go away to college or give community college a try; get a job or enlist in the military. Maybe you can convince your parents to bankroll an extended break to travel the world. Or, perhaps, you want to see what's out there by volunteering for a favorite cause or interning with an interesting company.

Of course, you may be one of the lucky few who have always known what they wanted to do with their lives—be a doctor, chef, or whatever. All you need to do is figure out a few wheres, whens, and hows to get you on your way. Get the training, master the skills, and off you go to fulfill your destiny.

On the other hand, you may be one of the hordes of high schoolers who have absolutely no clue what

1

they want to do with the rest of their lives. But—whatever—you'll just head off to college anyway. After all, everyone else is doing it. And, for that matter, everyone that matters seems to think that's what you're *supposed* to do.

But, here's the thing: College is pretty much a once-in-a-lifetime opportunity. Not to mention that it is a *very expensive* once-in-a-lifetime-opportunity. It's unlikely that you'll ever get another four years to step back from the rest of the world and totally focus on getting yourself ready to succeed in life. Assuming that you are way too smart to squander your best shot at success with aimless dabbling, you can use this book to make well-informed choices about your future.

A premise suggested by a famous guy named Noel Coward inspired the ultimate goal of this book. Coward was an English playwright who was born in 1899. After a colorful life working as a composer, director, actor, and singer, Coward concluded that interesting "work is more fun than fun." Making this statement true for you is what this book is all about.

Mind you, fun isn't limited to the ha-ha, goofing-off-with-friends variety. Sometimes it's best expressed as the big sigh of satisfaction people describe when they truly enjoy their life's work. It involves finding the kind of work that provides purpose to your days and a solid foundation for building a well-rounded life. You'll know you've found it when you look forward to Mondays almost as much as you do Fridays!

Need more convincing? Consider this: If you are like most people, you will spend a big chunk of the next 40 or 50 years of your life working. Sorry to break it to you like that but, well, welcome to the real world. Putting a little thought into how you really want to spend all that time kind of makes sense, doesn't it?

If you agree, you've come to the right place. In these pages you'll encounter a sequence of activities and strategies you can use—much like a compass—to find your way to a bright future. Each of the 16 titles in the *Career Ideas for Teens* series features the following three sections:

SECTION ONE: DISCOVER YOU AT WORK

It's your choice, your career, your future. Do you notice a common theme here? Yep, this first step is all about you. Stop here and

> **REALITY CHECK**
> News flash! Contrary to popular opinion, you cannot grow up to be anything you want to be. You can, however, grow up to be anything you are willing to work hard to become.

WHICH WAY SHOULD YOU GO?

Each of the 16 titles in the *Career Ideas for Teens* series focuses on a specific industry theme. Some people refer to these themes as career "clusters." Others call them career "pathways." Your school may even offer career academies based on one or more of these themes. Whatever you call them, they offer a terrific way to explore the entire world of work in manageable, easy-to-navigate segments. Explore *Career Ideas for Teens* in…

- Agriculture, Food, and Natural Resources
- Architecture and Construction
- Arts and Communications
- Business, Management, and Administration
- Education and Training
- Finance
- Government and Public Service
- Health Science
- Hospitality and Tourism
- Human Services
- Information Technology
- Law and Public Safety
- Manufacturing
- Marketing
- Science, Technology, Engineering, and Math
- Transportation, Distribution, and Logistics

think about what you really want to do. Better yet, stick around until you get a sense of the skills, interests, ambitions, and values you already possess that can take you places in the real world.

Sure, this first step can be a doozy. It's also one that many people miss. Just talk to the adults in your life about their career choices. Find out how many of them took the time to choose a career based on personal preferences and strengths. Then ask how many of them wish now that they had. You're likely to learn that if they had it to do over again, they would jump at the chance to make well-informed career choices.

SECTION TWO: EXPLORE YOUR OPTIONS

Next, come all the career ideas you'd expect to find in a book called *Career Ideas for Teens*. Each of the 35 careers featured in this section represents possible destinations along a career cluster pathway. With opportunities associated with 16 different career clusters—everything from agriculture and art to transportation and technology—you're sure to find intriguing new ideas to consider. Forget any preconceived notions about what you (or others) think you *should* be and take some time to figure out what you really want to be. Put all the things you discovered about yourself in Section One to good use as you explore the world of work.

SECTION THREE: EXPERIMENT WITH SUCCESS

What would it really be like to be a...whatever it is you want to be? Why wait until it's too late to change your mind to find out? Here's your chance to take career ideas of interest for a test drive. Play around with this one; give that one a try.... It's a no-pressure, no-obligation way to find work you really want to do.

This three-step process is about uncovering potential (yours) and possibilities (career paths). Plunge in, give it some thought, uncover the clues, put the pieces together...whatever it takes to find the way to your very best future!

DISCOVER YOU AT WORK

Sometimes people make things harder than they have to be. Like waiting until the night before a big exam to start studying.... Agonizing over asking a special someone to the prom instead of, um, just asking.... Worrying about finishing a project instead of sitting down and doing it....

Figuring out what you want to do with your life can be that way, too. Sure, it is a big decision. And, yes, the choices you make now can have a big impact on the rest of your life. But, there's good news. You don't have to figure everything out now.

Bottom line, every potential employer you are likely to encounter throughout your entire career will want to know two things: "What do you know?" and "What can you do?"

That being the case, what can you do to prepare for a successful career?

Two things: 1) Become a skilled expert in something that you like to do, and 2) find an employer willing to pay you to do it.

Really.

It's that simple...and that complicated.

"Me, Myself, and I" offers a starting point where you can uncover insightful clues about personal interests, skills, values, and ambitions you can use to make sound career decisions. Think through a round of who, what, when, where, how questions in "Me, Myself, and I" about you and then move on to "Hello, World of Work," where you'll discover how to match what you want from work with what specific types of skills employers need from you.

SOME GOOD ADVICE

"If you want an average successful life, it doesn't take much planning. Just stay out of trouble, go to school, and apply for jobs you might like. But if you want something extraordinary, you have two choices:

1. Become the best at one specific thing.
2. Become very good (top 25 percent) at two or more things.

The first strategy is difficult to the point of near impossibility. Few people will ever play in the NBA or make a platinum album. I don't recommend anyone even try.

The second strategy is fairly easy. Everyone has at least a few areas in which they could be in the top 25 percent with some effort. In my case, I can draw better than most people can, but I'm hardly an artist. And I'm not any funnier than the average standup comedian who never makes it big, but I'm funnier than most people. The magic is that few people can draw well and write jokes. It's the combination of the two that makes what I do so rare. And when you add in my business background, suddenly I had a topic that few cartoonists could hope to understand without living it."

—*Scott Adams,*
creator of the Dilbert *comic strip*

Me, Myself, and I

Why do I need to learn all this stuff? Chances are that at some point in the dozen or so years you have already spent in school you have asked this question a time or two. Come on. What can quadratic polynomials and the periodic table of elements possibly have to do with the rest of your life?

Among other things, your education is supposed to get you ready to succeed in the real world. Yes, all those grammar rules and mathematical mysteries will someday come in handy no matter what you end up doing. Nevertheless, more than all the facts and figures you've absorbed, the plan all along—from kindergarten to graduation—has been to make sure you learn how to learn.

If you know how to learn, you'll know how to seek out and acquire pretty much anything you need or want to know. Get the knowledge, gain the skills, and the resulting expertise is your ticket to a successful career.

As its title suggests, this chapter is all about you—and for a very good reason. Your traits, interests, skills, work style, and values offer important clues you can use to make important decisions about your future—for valid reasons with intention and purpose.

And, speaking of clues…

Think of yourself like a good mystery, but instead of sleuthing out whodunit, focus on collecting evidence about you. By the time you have completed the following six activities, you'll be ready to encounter the world of work on your own terms.

Discover #1: WHO Am I?
Discover #2: WHAT Do I Like to Do?
Discover #3: WHERE Does My Work Style Fit Best?
Discover #4: WHY Do My Work Values Matter?
Discover #5: HOW Ready Am I for the 21st-Century Workplace?
Discover #6: "Me" Résumé

ON SUCCESS
If you don't know what you want, how will you know when you get it?

ON LIFE DIRECTION
If you don't know where you are going, how will you know when you get there?

DISCOVER #1: WHO AM I?

Make a grid with three columns and six rows on a blank sheet of paper. Number each row from one to six.

- In the first row, write the three best words you'd use to describe yourself.
- In the second row, ask a good friend what three words they'd use to describe you.
- In the third row, ask a favorite teacher for three words that she thinks best describe you.
- In the fourth row, ask a coach, club adviser, youth leader, or other adult mentor to use three words to describe you.
- In the fifth row, ask a sibling or other young relative to take a crack at describing you.
- In the sixth row, ask a parent or trusted adult relative for three descriptive words about you.

You			
Friend			
Teacher			
Coach or mentor			
Sibling or young relative			
Parent or adult relative			

Discovery #1: I Am...

Look for common themes in the way that others see you and compare them with the way you see yourself. Include the words used most often to describe you to write an official, ready-for-*Merriam-Webster's-Dictionary* definition of you.

_____

_____

_____

DISCOVER #2: WHAT DO I LIKE TO DO?

Think fast! Use a blank sheet of paper to complete the following statements with the first answers that come to mind.

1 I like to _____ , _____ ,

and _____ .

2 I am really good at _____ ,

_____ , and _____ .

3 I totally suck at _____ , _____ ,

and _____ .

4 Something I can do for hours without getting bored is

_____ .

5 One thing that absolutely bores me to tears is

_____ .

6 My favorite subjects in school are _____ ,

_____ , and _____ .

7 In my free time, I especially like to _____ ,

_____ , and _____ .

8 Something I'd really like to learn how to do is

_____ .

9 Other people compliment me most often about

_____ .

Discovery #2: I Like...

Use your responses to the prompts above to create a list of your three top interests. See if you can identify off the top of your head at least three careers with a direct connection to each interest.

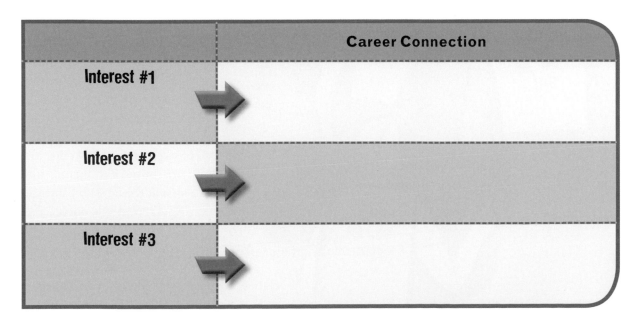

	Career Connection
Interest #1	
Interest #2	
Interest #3	

DISCOVER #3: WHERE DOES MY WORK STYLE FIT BEST?

It is your first day on the job and it's time for lunch. Walking into the employee cafeteria, you discover six tables. There is a big welcome sign instructing new employees to find the table that best matches his or her style. You quickly conclude that they aren't talking about preppy or retro fashions and start looking for other things you share in common. Read the following descriptions and choose the table where you fit in best.

Table 1: The Doers

These people do what it takes to get the job done, whether it involves building, fixing, or growing things, training people, or playing sports. They are practical, hands-on problem solvers who especially enjoy the great outdoors. Forget the paperwork and keep the human interaction to a minimum—these people would rather do something than talk about it. Among the colleagues seated at this table are an aerospace engineer, architect, carpenter, chef, civil engineer, park ranger, and police officer.

Table 2: The Thinkers

These people have never met a fact they didn't like. With a preference for tasks that require mental acuity over physical activity, you're likely to encounter as many laptops as lunchboxes here. Well known for insatiable curiosity, be prepared to answer lots of questions, discuss off-the-wall-subjects, and take a shot at the latest brainteaser circulating around the table. Feel free to strike up a conversation with your pick of an archaeologist, chiropractor, computer programmer, electrician, ecologist, psychologist, or zoologist.

ORGANIZER

HELPER

THINKER

DOER

CREATOR

PERSUADER

TAKE A SEAT!

A few things you'll want to know about these "lunch tables":

1. Each "table" represents one of the widely used Holland codes. This classification system was developed by psychologist Dr. John Holland as a way to link six distinct personality types to career choices and work success. The official work personality types include:
   - Doers = Realistic (R)
   - Thinkers = Investigative (I)
   - Creators = Artistic (A)
   - Helpers = Social (S)
   - Persuaders = Enterprising (E)
   - Organizers = Conventional (C)

2. There is no "best" work personality. It takes all kinds to keep the world working. When everything is in balance, there's a job for every person and a person for every job.
3. You, like most people, are probably a unique combination of more than one personality type: a little of this, a lot of that. That's what makes people interesting.

You can go online, plug in your work personality codes, and find lists of interest-related career options at http://online.onetcenter.org/find/descriptor/browse/Interests.

Table 3: The Creators

Here you'll find the artsy, free-spirit types—those drawn to words, art, and other forms of creative self-expression. Rules and structure tend to box in these out-of-the-box thinkers. Doing their own thing

WHAT'S YOUR STYLE?

ARE YOU A DOER?

Are you:
- Independent?
- Reserved?
- Practical?
- Mechanical?
- Athletic?
- Persistent?

Do you like:
- Building things?
- Training animals?
- Playing sports?
- Fixing things?
- Gardening?
- Hunting?
- Fishing?

ARE YOU A THINKER?

Are you:
- Logical?
- Independent?
- Analytical?
- Observant?
- Inquisitive?

Do you like:
- Exploring new subjects?
- Doing puzzles?
- Messing around with computers?
- Solving mysteries?
- Keeping up with the latest news and world events?
- Tackling new challenges?

ARE YOU A CREATOR?

Are you:
- Imaginative?
- Intuitive?
- Expressive?
- Emotional?
- Creative?
- Independent?

Do you like:
- Drawing?
- Painting?
- Playing an instrument?
- Visiting museums?
- Acting?
- Designing clothes ?
- Decorating spaces?
- Reading?
- Traveling?
- Writing?

ARE YOU A HELPER?

Are you:
- Friendly?
- Outgoing?
- Empathic?
- Persuasive?
- Idealistic?
- Generous?

Do you like:
- Joining clubs?
- Playing team sports?
- Caring for children?
- Going to parties?
- Meeting new people?

ARE YOU A PERSUADER?

Are you:
- Assertive?
- Self-confident?
- Ambitious?
- Extroverted?
- Optimistic?
- Adventurous?

Do you like:
- Organizing parties and other events?
- Selling things?
- Promoting ideas?
- Giving speeches?
- Starting businesses?

ARE YOU AN ORGANIZER?

Are you:
- Well-organized?
- Accurate?
- Practical?
- Persistent?
- Conscientious?
- Ambitious?

Do you like:
- Working with numbers?
- Collecting or organizing things?
- Proofreading?
- Keeping records?
- Keeping yourself and others on track?

MY WORK STYLE(S) IS...

- ❏ Doer (Realistic)
- ❏ Thinker (Investigative)
- ❏ Creator (Artistic)
- ❏ Helper (Social)
- ❏ Persuader (Enterprising)
- ❏ Organizer (Conventional)

is what they do best. Among your potential lunch companions are an actor, cartoon animator, choreographer, drama teacher, fashion designer, graphic designer, interior designer, journalist, and writer.

Table 4: Helpers

Good luck trying to get a word in edgewise at this table. Helpers are "people" people: always ready for a good chat or to lend a helping hand. Communicating with others trumps working with objects, machines, or data. They are all about serving people, promoting learning, and making the world a better place. Sit down and get acquainted with an arbitrator, art therapist, childcare worker, coach, counselor, cruise director, fitness trainer, registered nurse, and teacher.

Table 5: The Persuaders

While helpers focus on helping people, persuaders are natural leaders or managers—especially adept at getting people to do what they want them to do. These people are more about action than analysis, equally comfortable with taking risks and responsibility. Entrepreneurs at heart, they like to make things happen. Sit down and find your place among peers such as an advertising executive, criminal investigator, lawyer, lobbyist, school principal, stockbroker, and urban planner.

Table 6: The Organizers

Organizers are people you can count on to cross their t's and dot their i's. In other words, no detail escapes their careful attention. Most comfortable doing things "by the book," organizers thrive on routine and structure. A penchant for following instructions and respecting authority gives these types something of a squeaky-clean reputation. Make yourself comfortable and enjoy a nice break with an accountant, actuary, air traffic controller, chief financial officer, economist, mathematician, and paralegal.

DISCOVER #4: WHY DO MY WORK VALUES MATTER?

There's another thing to consider before evaluating all of the clues you've gathered. According to O*Net OnLine, America's primary source of occupational information, six types of values are commonly associated with workplace satisfaction: achievement, independence, recognition, relationships, support, and working conditions. Read each of the following statements and put an X in the box preceding those that are important to you.

In considering my future career, it matters most that

❑ **1.** I make use of my abilities.

❑ **2.** I can try out my own ideas.

❑ **3.** I can give directions and instructions to others.

❑ **4.** I would never be pressured to do things that go against my sense of right and wrong.

❑ **5.** I would be treated fairly by the company.

❑ **6.** The job would provide for steady employment.

❑ **7.** I enjoy the satisfaction of a job well done.

❑ **8.** I can make decisions on my own.

❑ **9.** I could receive recognition for the work I do.

❑ **10.** I could do things for other people.

❑ **11.** I have supervisors who would support their workers with management.

❑ **12.** My pay would compare well with that of other workers.

❑ **13.** What I do matters.

❑ **14.** I can work with little supervision.

❑ **15.** The job would provide an opportunity for advancement.

❑ **16.** My coworkers would be easy to get along with.

❑ **17.** I have supervisors who train their workers well.

❑ **18.** The job would have good working conditions.

☐ **19.** I find a sense of accomplishment in my work.

☐ **20.** I have some flexibility in when and how I do my work.

☐ **21.** My work efforts are appreciated.

☐ **22.** I have the opportunity to work with all kinds of people.

☐ **23.** My work expectations are clearly defined and necessary resources are provided.

☐ **24.** I could do something different every day.

Tally up your results here.

Achievement	Independence	Recognition
☐ 1	☐ 2	☐ 3
☐ 7	☐ 8	☐ 9
☐ 13	☐ 14	☐ 15
☐ 19	☐ 20	☐ 21
Total	**Total**	**Total**
Relationships	**Support**	**Working Conditions**
☐ 4	☐ 5	☐ 6
☐ 10	☐ 11	☐ 12
☐ 16	☐ 17	☐ 18
☐ 22	☐ 23	☐ 24
Total	**Total**	**Total**

Your Work Values at Work

Once you've clued yourself in to what's important to you in a career, you need to connect those values to actual jobs.

Achievement: If Achievement is your highest work value, look for jobs that let you use your best abilities. Look for work where you can see the results of your efforts. Explore jobs where you can get a genuine sense of accomplishment.

Independence: If Independence is your highest work value, look for jobs where employers let you do things on your own initiative. Explore work where you can make decisions on your own.

Recognition: If Recognition is your highest work value, explore jobs that come with good possibilities for advancement. Look for work with prestige or with the potential for leadership.

Relationships: If Relationships are your highest work value, look for jobs where your coworkers are friendly. Look for work that lets you be of service to others. Explore jobs that do not make you do anything that goes against your sense of right and wrong.

Support: If Support is your highest work value, look for jobs where the company stands behind its workers and where supervision is handled in supportive ways. Explore work in companies with a reputation for competent, considerate, and fair management.

Working Conditions: If Working Conditions are your highest work value, consider pay, job security, and good working conditions when looking at jobs. Look for work that suits your work style. Some people like to be busy all the time, or work alone, or have many different things to do.

Discovery #4: My Work Values Include
- ❑ Achievement
- ❑ Independence
- ❑ Recognition
- ❑ Relationships
- ❑ Support
- ❑ Working Conditions

DISCOVER #5: HOW READY AM I FOR THE 21ST-CENTURY WORKPLACE?

Are you ready for the 21st-century workforce? Some of America's most prominent employers and educators want to make sure. They put their heads together and came up with a list of essential skills, called 21st-century skills, which they recommend you bring to your first big job.

Some of these skills you've been busy acquiring without even knowing it. For instance, every time you go online to play games or do a little social networking you are cultivating important technology skills. Other skills will take some work. You can find an official description of these skills at http://www.p21.org. In the meantime, you can do a very informal assessment of your workplace skills using this 21st-century skills meter.

21st-CENTURY SKILLS METER

On the following scales, 1 represents total cluelessness, 10 represents impressive competency of the straight-A variety, and 2–9 represent varying degrees in between.

How would you describe your mastery of the following subject:

	1	2	3	4	5	6	7	8	9	10
English, reading, and language arts?										
Foreign language?										
Arts?										
Mathematics?										
Economics?										
Science?										
Geography?										
History?										
Government and civics?										

How would you rate your current knowledge about:

	1	2	3	4	5	6	7	8	9	10
Global issues?										
Other cultures, religions, and lifestyles?										
Managing your personal finances?										
Understanding the world of work?										
Using entrepreneurial skills to enhance workplace productivity and career options?										

(continues)

21st-CENTURY SKILLS METER (continued)

	1	2	3	4	5	6	7	8	9	10
Local and national political events?										
Being part of the democratic process?										
Making good choices about your health and wellness?										
How good are you at:										
Making good decisions using sound judgment based on careful evaluation of evidence and ideas?										
Solving problems using both common sense and innovative ideas?										
Communicating thoughts and ideas verbally?										
Communicating thoughts and ideas in writing?										
Using various types of media and technology to inform, instruct, motivate, and/or persuade?										
Collaborating with others and working as a team?										

21st-CENTURY SKILLS METER										
	1	2	3	4	5	6	7	8	9	10
Finding information in a wide variety of ways that includes books, newspapers, the Internet, etc.?										
Quickly learning how to use new technologies such as smart phones and online games?										
Getting used to new situations and finding the middle ground in disagreements?										
Thinking "out of the box" in creative and innovative ways?										
Understanding world issues and global cultures?										
Finding ways to protect and sustain the earth's environment?										

Discovery #5: I Am Getting Ready for the 21st-Century Workforce...

Use the two columns below to list skills you are already actively cultivating (those you scored 6 or higher) and those you need to take steps to pursue (those you scored 5 or lower).

In Progress	In Pursuit

DISCOVER #6: "ME" RÉSUMÉ

Eventually you will need to put together a job-hunting résumé that presents in a concise and compelling way all the reasons an employer should hire you. But, you aren't looking for a job right now. You are looking for a future.

It just so happens that creating a résumé with a twist offers a great way to make sense of all the fascinating facts you've just discovered about yourself. It also offers the double-whammy benefit of practicing your résumé-writing skills. So use the following format to create a "me" résumé summarizing what you've just learned about yourself in a professional way.

NAME

I am...

(* Put the definition of you here)

I like...

(* Key interests)

I work best...

(* Work style)

I most value...

(* Work values)

I am getting ready for the 21st-century workforce...

(* 21st-century skills already acquired and in process)

Hello, World of Work

Pop quiz!

What are the two things necessary for finding a successful career?

Hint #1: You started thinking about some interesting options for one of these "ingredients" in "Me, Myself, and I."

Hint #2: You are about to find out how to find the second ingredient in "Hello, World of Work."

Give yourself an A+ if your answer is anything like

1 Become an expert in something that you like to do, and
2 Find an employer who is willing to pay you to do it.

Finding a career you want to pursue is only half the challenge. The flipside involves finding out what the world of work wants from you. Keep the clues you discovered about yourself in the "Me, Myself, and I" section in the back of your mind as the focus shifts from self-discovery to work-discovery.

It's a big world out there—finding a path where you can get where you want to go is the next order of business.

DISCOVER #7: WHERE CAN MY INTERESTS AND SKILLS TAKE ME?

First, a confession: The following interest inventory is intended for use as an informal career exploration tool. It makes no claims of scientific validity or statistical reliability.

It was inspired by (and used with permission of) the Career Clusters Interest Survey developed by the States' Career Clusters Initiative, and the Oklahoma Department of Career and Technology Education. It includes significant revisions, however, that are meant to offer an age-appropriate, self-discovery tool to teens like you.

Your school guidance office can provide information about formal assessment and aptitude resources you may want to use at some point. In the meantime, use this informal interest inventory to start your exploration process and to make the connection between you and the world of work.

Following are eight different lists representing diverse interests that range from childhood play preferences to save-the-world ambitions. Each type of interest offers unique insight about career paths that may take you where you want to go in life.

Read each question and choose the response(s) that are most true for you.

When you were a little kid, what was your favorite thing to do?

❑ **1.** Play outside, explore nature, plan big adventures.

❑ **2.** Build things with Lego's, Lincoln logs, or other construction sets.

❑ **3.** Put on plays to entertain your family and friends.

❑ **4.** Run a lemonade stand.

❑ **5.** Pretend you were a teacher and play school.

❑ **6.** Play storekeeper and run the cash register with phony money.

❑ **7.** Pretend you were president of the United States or boss of the world.

❑ **8.** Play doctor and nurse your stuffed animals and siblings back to health.

❑ **9.** Get your friends and neighbors together for backyard games, obstacle courses, or secret clubs.

❑ **10.** Take care of stray animals, play with pets, pet-sit for neighbors.

❑ **11.** Play Nintendo, Game Boy, or other kinds of video games.

❑ **12.** Take turns being the "bad guy" in cops and robbers or use a spy kit to collect fingerprints and other clues.

❑ **13.** Build model planes or cars or come up with new inventions.

❑ **14.** Do arts and crafts.

❏ **15.** Concoct new formulas with a junior chemistry set.

❏ **16.** Play with cars, trucks, and trains, and build roads and bridges.

Which of the following lists of subjects would you most like to study?

❏ **1.** Biology, botany, chemistry, ecology, horticulture, zoology.

❏ **2.** Art, computer-aided design, drafting, construction trades, geometry.

❏ **3.** Art, broadcasting, creative writing, graphic design, journalism, music, theater arts.

❏ **4.** Accounting, business, cooperative education, economics, information technology.

❏ **5.** Child development, family and consumer studies, psychology, social studies, sociology.

❏ **6.** Accounting, business law, business math, economics, personal finance.

❏ **7.** Civics and government, current events, debate, foreign language, history, philosophy.

❏ **8.** Biology, chemistry, health, math, occupational health, language arts.

❏ **9.** Culinary arts, food service, foreign language, geography, language arts, speech.

❏ **10.** Anthropology, family and consumer science, foreign language, language arts, psychology, sociology.

❏ **11.** Communication, computer applications, graphic design, math, science, technology education.

❏ **12.** First aid, forensic science, government, health, history, language arts, law enforcement, psychology.

❏ **13.** Chemistry, geometry, language arts, physics, shop, trades.

❏ **14.**   Business education, computer applications, distributive education, economics, language arts, marketing.

❏ **15.**   Computer-aided design, computer networking, drafting, electronics, engineering, math, science.

❏ **16.**   Economics, foreign language, math, physical science, trade and industry.

Which type of afterschool club or activity are you more likely to join?

❏ **1.**   4-H, Future Farmers of America (FFA), community gardening.

❏ **2.**   Habitat for Humanity, construction club, trade apprenticeship.

❏ **3.**   Dance, drama, chorus, marching band, newspaper staff, yearbook staff.

❏ **4.**   Future Business Leaders of America (FBLA), Junior Achievement.

❏ **5.**   National Honor Society, peer-to-peer mentor, tutor.

❏ **6.**   Stock Market Game, investment club.

❏ **7.**   Student government, debate team.

❏ **8.**   Sports trainer, Health Occupations Students of America (HOSA), Red Cross volunteer.

❏ **9.**   Culture Club, International Club, Model United Nations Club.

❏ **10.**   Beta Club; Key Club; Family, Career and Community Leaders of America (FCCLA).

❏ **11.**   High-Tech Club, Technology Student Association (TSA), Video Gamers Club.

❏ **12.**   Law Enforcement Explorer Post.

❏ **13.**   Odyssey of the Mind, SkillsUSA/Vocational Industrial Clubs of America (VICA).

❏ **14.**   Distributive Education Clubs of America (DECA) Marketing Club, junior fashion advisory board.

- ❑ **15.** Junior Engineering Technical Society (JETS), math club, National High School Science Bowl, science club.
- ❑ **16.** Environmental awareness clubs, National High School Solar Car Race.

Which of the following weekend activities would you most enjoy doing?

- ❑ **1.** Fishing, hunting, or hiking.
- ❑ **2.** Building a house for a needy family with Habitat for Humanity.
- ❑ **3.** Going to a concert or to see the latest movie.
- ❑ **4.** Getting a part-time job.
- ❑ **5.** Volunteering at the library or reading stories to children at a homeless shelter.
- ❑ **6.** Staying up all night playing Monopoly with friends.
- ❑ **7.** Working on a favorite political candidate's election campaign.
- ❑ **8.** Hosting a big birthday bash for a friend.
- ❑ **9.** Helping out at the local Ronald McDonald House or children's hospital.
- ❑ **10.** Taking a Red Cross first aid course or disaster-relief course.
- ❑ **11.** Playing a new video game or setting up a new home page for social networking.
- ❑ **12.** Watching all your favorite cop shows on TV.
- ❑ **13.** Giving your room an eco-makeover.
- ❑ **14.** Making posters to celebrate homecoming or a big school event.
- ❑ **15.** Competing in a local science fair.
- ❑ **16.** Building a soapbox derby car to race with friends.

Which of the following group of words best describes you?

- [ ] **1.** Adventurous, eco-friendly, outdoorsy, physically active.
- [ ] **2.** Artistic, curious, detail oriented, patient, persistent, visual thinker.
- [ ] **3.** Creative, determined, dramatic, imaginative, talkative, tenacious.
- [ ] **4.** Logical, natural leader, practical, organized, responsible, tactful.
- [ ] **5.** Attentive, decisive, friendly, helpful, innovative, inquisitive.
- [ ] **6.** Efficient, good with numbers, logical, methodical, orderly, self-confident, trustworthy.
- [ ] **7.** Articulate, competitive, organized, persuasive, problem-solver, service minded.
- [ ] **8.** Attentive, careful, caring, compassionate, conscientious, patient, task oriented.
- [ ] **9.** Adventurous, easygoing, fun loving, outgoing, self-motivated, tactful.
- [ ] **10.** Accepting, attentive, articulate, intuitive, logical, sensible, thrifty.
- [ ] **11.** Accurate, analytical, detail oriented, focused, logical, persistent, precise, technology whiz.
- [ ] **12.** Adventurous, community minded, courageous, dependable, decisive, fair, optimistic.
- [ ] **13.** Active, coordinated, inquisitive, observant, practical, steady.
- [ ] **14.** Competitive, creative, enthusiastic, persuasive, self-motivated.
- [ ] **15.** Curious about how things work, detail oriented, inquisitive, objective, mechanically inclined, observant.
- [ ] **16.** Coordinated, mechanical, multitasker, observant, prepared, realistic.

If you could do only one thing to make the world a better place, which of the following would you do?

❑ **1.** Eliminate hunger everywhere.

❑ **2.** Create sustainable, eco-friendly environments.

❑ **3.** Keep the world entertained and informed.

❑ **4.** Provide meaningful jobs and fair trade opportunities for everyone.

❑ **5.** Teach the world to read so that no one is limited by a lack of education.

❑ **6.** Keep national and global financial systems on track.

❑ **7.** Promote world peace and stable governments for all.

❑ **8.** Provide access to high-quality health care services for everyone.

❑ **9.** Bridge cultural differences through communication and collaboration.

❑ **10.** Help people in need get back on their feet.

❑ **11.** Use technology to solve the world's most pressing problems.

❑ **12.** Make the world a safer place where justice prevails.

❑ **13.** Discover a new innovation on par with Edison's invention of electricity that has the potential to improve the quality of life for all mankind.

❑ **14.** Get the word out about a favorite issue or cause.

❑ **15.** Find a cure for cancer, AIDS, or other life-threatening disease.

❑ **16.** Develop more efficient ways to get people and things where they need to go.

Which of the following lists of career options intrigues you most?

❑ **1.** Agricultural economist, botanist, food broker, food scientist, forester, geologist, hydrologist, nutritionist, recycler, wastewater manager.

❑ **2.** Civil engineer, demolition technician, energy-efficient builder, heavy-equipment operator, landscape architect, urban planner.

❑ **3.** Actor, blogger, commercial artist, digital media specialist, museum curator, social medial consultant, stage manager, writer.

❑ **4.** Advertising account executive, brand manager, budget analyst, chief executive officer, dispatcher, e-commerce analyst, green entrepreneur, international businessperson, purchasing agent.

❑ **5.** Animal trainer, coach, college professor, corporate trainer, guidance counselor, principal, speech pathologist, textbook publisher.

❑ **6.** Accountant, banker, chief financial officer, economist, fraud investigator, investment adviser, property manager, stock broker, wealth manager.

❑ **7.** Bank examiner, city planner, customs agent, federal special agent, intelligence analyst, politician, private investigator.

❑ **8.** Art therapist, audiologist, chiropractor, dentist, massage therapist, pharmacist, surgeon, veterinarian.

❑ **9.** Banquet manager, chef, cruise ship captain, exhibit designer, golf pro, resort manager, theme park designer, tour guide, wedding planner.

❑ **10.** Career coach, child care director, elder care center manager, hairstylist, personal trainer, psychologist, religious leader, teacher, victim advocate.

- ❏ **11.** Artificial intelligence scientist, chief information officer, computer forensics investigator, database modeler, e-commerce entrepreneur, Webmaster.
- ❏ **12.** Animal control officer, coroner, detective, emergency medical technician, firefighter, lawyer, park ranger, warden, wildlife conservation officer.
- ❏ **13.** Chemical engineer, hybrid car designer, industrial designer, logistician, millwright, nanotechnologist, robotics technologist, traffic engineer, welder.
- ❏ **14.** Art designer, business development manager, copywriter, creative director, graphic designer, market researcher, media buyer, new media specialist, retail store manager, social media consultant.
- ❏ **15.** Aeronautical engineer, anthropologist, chemist, ecologist, telecommunications engineer, mathematician, oceanographer, zoologist.
- ❏ **16.** Air traffic controller, cargo inspector, flight attendant, logistics planner, pilot, railroad engineer, surveyor, truck driver.

Which of the following types of work environments would you most like to work in?

- ❏ **1.** Farm, food processing plant, food science laboratory, forest, garden center, greenhouse, national park, recycling center.
- ❏ **2.** Construction site, commercial facilities, government agency, corporate office, private firm, residential properties.
- ❏ **3.** Independent, creative business, museum, news agency, publishing company, studio, theater.
- ❏ **4.** Business planning office, corporate headquarters, government agency, international business center.

❑   **5.**   College counseling center, elementary school, high school, middle school, museum, preschool, school district office.

❑   **6.**   Accounting firm, bank, brokerage firm, corporate office, insurance company, stock market.

❑   **7.**   Business development office, chamber of commerce, city/county/state/federal government agency; courthouse; law firm.

❑   **8.**   Dental office, hospital, medical research center, pharmacy, physician's office, surgical complex, urgent care center, veterinary clinic.

❑   **9.**   Airport, amusement park, hotel, public park, resort, restaurant, sports center, travel agency, zoo.

❑   **10.**   Employment agency, consumer credit bureau, elder care center, fitness center, mental health care center, real estate office, school, spa.

❑   **11.**   Corporation, information technology company, new media development center, research and development laboratory, small business.

❑   **12.**   Courthouse, prison, fire station, government agency, law firm, national park, police station.

❑   **13.**   Manufacturing plant, design firm, engineering company, production facility, research and development laboratory.

❑   **14.**   Advertising agency, independent creative business, corporate marketing department, retail store, new media development center.

❑   **15.**   Science laboratory, engineering firm, information technology company, research and development center.

❑   **16.**   Airport, marina, mass transit authority, railroad, shipping port, subway system, transportation center.

Go back through your answers and record how many of each of the following numbers you have marked.

1s	2s	3s	4s	5s	6s	7s	8s
9s	10s	11s	12s	13s	14s	15s	16s

Discovery #7: My Interests and Skills...

What do your answers say about your personal preferences, natural inclinations, and ambitions? In what ways can you use these clues to better inform your career choices? What general direction are your skills and interests pointing toward? Describe below.

_____

_____

_____

_____

_____

DISCOVER #8: WHICH CAREER PATH IS RIGHT FOR ME?

If you had more...	Consider this career cluster...	To explore careers that involve...
1s	Agriculture, Food, and Natural Resources	Producing, processing, marketing, distributing, financing, and developing agricultural commodities and resources including food, fiber, wood products, natural resources, horticulture, and other plant and animal products and resources.
2s	Architecture and Construction	Designing, planning, managing, building, and maintaining the built environment.
3s	Arts, A/V Technology, and Communications	Designing, producing, exhibiting, performing, writing, and publishing multimedia content including visual and performing arts and design, journalism, and entertainment services.
4s	Business, Management, and Administration	Planning, organizing, directing, and evaluating business functions essential to efficient and productive business operations.
5s	Education and Training	Planning, managing, and providing education and training services, and related learning support services.
6s	Finance	Planning services for financial and investment planning, banking, insurance, and business financial management.
7s	Government and Public Service	Governing, planning, regulating, managing, and administering governmental functions at the local, state, and federal levels.
8s	Health Science	Planning, managing, and providing therapeutic services, diagnostic services, health informatics, support services, and biotechnology research and development.

(continues)

(continued)

If you had more...	Consider this career cluster...	To explore careers that involve...
9s	Hospitality and Tourism	Managing, marketing, and operating restaurants and other food services, lodging, attractions, recreation events, and travel-related services.
10s	Human Services	Preparing individuals for employment in career pathways that relate to families and human needs.
11s	Information Technology	Designing, developing, supporting, and managing hardware, software, multimedia, and systems integration services.
12s	Law, Public Safety, Corrections, and Security	Planning, managing, and providing legal, public safety, protective services, and homeland security, including professional and technical support services.
13s	Manufacturing	Planning, managing, and performing the processing of materials into intermediate or final products and related professional and technical support activities.
14s	Marketing	Planning, managing, and performing marketing activities to reach organizational objectives.
15s	Science, Technology, Engineering, and Mathematics	Planning, managing, and providing scientific research and professional and technical services including laboratory and testing services, and research and development services.
16s	Transportation, Distribution, and Logistics	Planning, managing, and moving of people, materials, and goods by road, pipeline, air, rail, and water, and related professional and technical support services.

Gratefully adapted and used with permission from the States' Career Clusters Initiative.

Discovery #8: My Career Path

With all scores tallied and all interests considered, where should you begin exploring your future career? List the three career clusters you most want to explore here:

1 _____

2 _____

3 _____

As you can probably guess, each title in the *Career Ideas for Teens* series is based on one of the career clusters described above. For the most effective career exploration process, start with the title most in sync with both your assessment results and your gut instincts about what you want to do with your life.

No matter which title you choose, be prepared to encounter exciting opportunities you've never considered—maybe even some you've never heard of before. You may find that your interests, skills, and ambitions lead you to a specific career idea that inspires your immediate plans for the future. On the other hand, those same interests, skills, and ambitions may simply point you toward a particular pathway or industry segment such as agriculture or education. That's just fine, too. Time, experience, opportunities—and the "Experiment with Success" activities you'll encounter in Section Three—will eventually converge to get you right where you want to be.

If you scored high in and are especially curious about...	Start exploring career options in Section Two of...
Agriculture, Food, and Natural Resources	*Career Ideas for Teens in Agriculture, Food, and Natural Resources*
Architecture and Construction	*Career Ideas for Teens in Architecture and Construction, Second Edition*
Arts, A/V Technology, and Communications	*Career Ideas for Teens in the Arts and Communications, Second Edition*
Business, Management, and Administration	*Career Ideas for Teens in Business, Management, and Administration*
Education and Training	*Career Ideas for Teens in Education and Training, Second Edition*
Finance	*Career Ideas for Teens in Finance*
Government and Public Service	*Career Ideas for Teens in Government and Public Service, Second Edition*
Health Science	*Career Ideas for Teens in Health Science, Second Edition*
Hospitality and Tourism	*Career Ideas for Teens in Hospitality and Tourism*
Human Services	*Career Ideas for Teens in Human Services*
Information Technology	*Career Ideas for Teens in Information Technology, Second Edition*
Law, Public Safety, Corrections, and Security	*Career Ideas for Teens in Law and Public Safety, Second Edition*
Manufacturing	*Career Ideas for Teens in Manufacturing, Second Edition*
Marketing	*Career Ideas for Teens in Marketing*
Science, Technology, Engineering, and Mathematics	*Career Ideas for Teens in Science, Technology, Engineering, and Math*
Transportation, Distribution, and Logistics	*Career Ideas for Teens in Transportation, Distribution, and Logistics*

DISCOVER #9: CAREER RÉSUMÉ

In "Me, Myself, and I," you summarized all your discoveries in a "me" résumé. This time, shift the focus to create a career résumé that describes what you currently consider a "dream job." Use a blend of your own wants and opportunities you'd expect to find along your favorite career path to fill in the categories below.

Career Title _____

_____

Job Description _____

_____

_____

Skills Needed _____

_____

_____

Knowledge Required _____

_____

_____

Work Environment _____

_____

_____

Perks and Benefits _____

_____

_____

MOVING ON

Ready to start exploring career ideas? Section Two is where potential and possibilities meet. As you start exploring options associated with this career path, look for those careers that best match the discoveries you've made about yourself. Make sure any opportunity you decide to pursue matches up with all you've just learned about your ambitions, skills, interests, values, and work style.

EXPLORE YOUR OPTIONS

If you are looking for a "safe" and varied career field, business is as safe and varied as it gets. Every possible type of industry you can imagine relies on similar business principles to function and prosper, which means that people with solid business skills can, in a sense, have their cake and eat it too. For instance, an accountant can choose to work in any business that needs sound financial practices or he can choose to put his number-crunching abilities to work in an industry of particular interest. A sports enthusiast might seek out accounting jobs with professional sports teams, sports equipment manufacturers, and so on.

Mixing business with pleasure is just one of the reasons to give this field a serious look. Demand is another reason. Every industry needs well-trained people who can organize, plan, and manage their way to success. The number of options for specialization within this field also makes it appealing. Accounting, finance, human resources, marketing, nonprofit management, leadership, and real estate are just a few of the areas of specialization business majors can choose. Again, it's another way professionals can match their own skills and interests with opportunities in business.

The next section introduces some of these options according to six different pathways. These pathways, as defined by the States' Career Clusters Project (an initiative of the National Association of State Directors of Career Technical Education Consortium) include: Management, Business Financial Management and Accounting, Human Resources, Business Analysis, Marketing, and Administration and Information Support. Getting acquainted with the following pathways can help you sort through the options and focus in on those most suited to your personal goals, interests, and strengths.

MANAGEMENT

Here you'll find a wide variety of job titles, all of which, in varying degrees, can best be defined as "boss." Chief executive officer (CEO) tops the list as leader of an entire corporation. Director, manager, and vice president are other job titles associated with managing companies, departments, divisions, and other types of business operations. A college degree in business will get you started along this pathway, but a master of business administration (MBA) opens the door to opportunities at higher levels of responsibility.

BUSINESS FINANCIAL MANAGEMENT AND ACCOUNTING

Accountant, adjuster, auditor, bookkeeper, price analyst, treasurer, billing clerk, and finance director are among the number-crunching opportunities found along this pathway. Chief financial officer (CFO) is the title given to the person with the ultimate financial decision-making responsibilities for a company or corporation. These professions typically require a degree in accounting or finance. There are additional opportunities for those who take on the extra step of licensure as a certified public accountant (CPA).

HUMAN RESOURCES

As the name of this pathway implies, human resources (HR) deals with the people side of business. Jobs in this pathway are associated with taking care of the employees of a business: recruiting and hiring them, training them, handling benefits and compensation matters, monitoring labor and other compliance issues, and more.

BUSINESS ANALYSIS

Business analysts, whether their job is involved with budgets, compensation, cost, databases, finances, investments, management, marketing, projects, or systems, are the "thinkers" within a business entity. According to experts with the States' Career Clusters Project, the business analyst's job is to "research and study business data to create solutions that are most cost-effective and beneficial to the business while promoting its philosophies and strategies." Tools of this trade include statistics, data, and other sources of client and product information.

MARKETING

Promoting and selling a company's products and services is the bottom-line goal of a wide variety of marketing occupations that includes everything from marketing and public relations mangers

A NOTE ON WEB SITES

Web sites tend to move around a bit. If you have trouble finding a specific site referred to in the following career profiles, use a favorite search engine to search for a specific Web site or type of information.

to retail clerks and telemarketers. The U.S. Department of Labor predicts growing numbers of opportunities in the areas of sales and service.

ADMINISTRATION AND INFORMATION SUPPORT

Administration and information support professionals perform the functions that keep businesses organized and running efficiently. Among the job titles associated with this pathway are administrative assistant, medical records clerk, office manager, paralegal, receptionist, and word processor.

Advertising Account Manager

You've got a client on the phone, your second line is beeping, your computer screen shows 33 unread messages (and it's only 9:15 A.M.), the head of the creative team is standing impatiently at your desk with some new print ad proposals, and you have a budget meeting in 45 seconds. To say an account executive's job at an ad agency is fast-paced and hectic is like saying lava is warm to the touch. But, if you're the kind of person who thrives under pressure, you won't want to be anywhere else.

When a company decides it needs to market one of its products or services, it often turns to an ad agency to get the job done. (Yes, most of those jingles touting the best cola to drink and those flashing Web site banners with discounts on your next purchase of running shoes are created by advertising agencies.) The agency works within a budget and under deadlines to assess how to best advertise the company's product or service, and then, once approved by the client, implements that strategy.

The account executive is the central organizational hub for one or more of an agency's clients. You don't create the ads (though

GET STARTED NOW!

- In School: English, writing classes, advanced computer courses, accounting, and any courses related to marketing or media.
- After School: Yearbook (seek to become manager or editor in chief), literary magazine, and computer clubs.
- Around Town: Keep a journal of clever advertising campaigns you see in your neighborhood, on television, and online.

depending on the agency, you may be an integral part of the brainstorming strategy meetings); however, if the client has a problem, they call you. If one of the teams working on your client's campaign is unsure of the direction or needs something approved by the client, they shoot you an e-mail. In short, it's your job to organize the day-to-day running of each of your clients' advertising campaigns and make sure that not only is the work getting done (on time and within budget), but that each client is well informed of your agency's progress and, well, happy.

Your duties entail, but are not exclusive to, setting and managing campaign budgets, trafficking all campaign materials to your superiors and your clients, setting up and organizing meetings, contacting your clients (often daily), working with account managers and others on wooing potential new clients, coordinating the efforts of the different teams working on your clients' campaigns, writing reports, and monitoring the effectiveness of ongoing campaigns your agency has implemented for your clients.

As an account executive, you'll rely heavily on your organizational, communication, and presentation skills, as well as your ability to thrive under stressful situations—especially as deadlines loom. Your colleagues will look to you for clear guidance and strong organizational structures so they can do their jobs faster and better. Your clients turn to you for information, results, reassurance, and a relationship based on mutual trust and respect. Happy customers and coworkers, along with successful campaigns, will keep you in the spotlight (in a good way!), and you may soon find yourself with more, and bigger, clients. Then, watch out advertising world! Here you come.

Auditor

You walk into the office for the first time and workers you've never met before suddenly get very quiet. Concerned and angry faces look up and then move quickly back to their computer screens. Nightmare scenario? Not by a long shot. In fact, you look forward to the stares and whispers because they're your cue to get to work. You're not the CEO or even a cop; you're the numbers detective—the auditor.

Accountants are passionate about numbers. They can whip up charts and make sense of balance sheets in the blink of an eye. Their job is to create the company's financial statements and records and get the taxes paid on time. Auditors are accountants who surely enjoy their number crunching; however, it's not their job to keep the books. Instead, auditors make sure the accountants did their job well and correctly (hence the suspicion some employees express about auditors). As an auditor, you analyze and interpret the company's records on their assets, net worth, liabilities, income, expenses, taxes, and more, and then prepare a report on how accurate the statements are, how well the company is doing, and whether or not there's any wasteful spending or even illegal activity going on.

GET STARTED NOW!

- In School: Accounting, math, as well as any economic courses that cover financial markets, banking, and analyzing financial data.
- After School: Run for class treasurer or volunteer to be treasurer of your favorite after school club. Join a local Junior Achievement program (http://www.ja.org).
- Around Town: Apply for summer intern positions at accounting firms.

IF YOU WERE. . .

As an auditor about to audit a large, automobile manufacturer, how would you go about preparing for your audit?

. . . MAKE IT REAL!

Pick your favorite automobile company. Create a written report that analyzes the auto industry and the company's place within that industry. Are they the industry leaders or are they playing catch-up due to financial mismanagement and bad product decisions? Use the Internet to find up-to-date news stories. Find the company's annual report at its corporate Web site. Then write down your suggestions on how to make the company more profitable through cost-cutting measures and other means.

When hired to audit a company, your first obligation is to learn about the company and the kind of business it does. What financial regulations does it operate under? What does the company wish to accomplish over the next year or even five years? Next, you begin looking into how the company operates. How effective is it in paying its bills and organizing its payment systems? Then, you collect the financial statements and analyze them. Were the correct accounting procedures followed? Is all the money where it's supposed to be? Is the company in compliance with current tax laws? Along the way, you may encounter mistakes, wasteful spending, misuse of funds, or even stealing. Finally, you create a report for the company's management team that evaluates the records, confirms or challenges their reliability, and then offers guidelines for improvements as well as advice on creating stronger systems and cost-saving measures.

So as you can see, it takes way more than a calculator to audit a company. Whether you're an internal auditor working directly for a company or an external one brought in by the company in order to prove to shareholders or potential investors that they're running a good business, it's your job to be fair, accurate, objective, and trusting in your own judgment. As you hone your research skills, analytical abilities, and number-crunching prowess, it will be your knack for knowing how to ask questions without sounding accusatory and approaching suspicious employees in a way that encourages cooperation that will bring you the greatest success as an auditor.

Brand Manager

Norbert, a (fictional) multinational manufacturer of electronic media devices, has decided to create a new line of products—sturdy toy cameras for young children that take real digital photographs. These products need a lot more than names to attract people to buy them. They need advertising, packaging, a message, and even a personality—in short, they need a brand. All the major products have one: Pepsi, Coke, Apple, Nike, etc. This brand has to make these cameras stand out from the competition and from all the other products demanding people's attention. And the person who has to make all of this happen is the brand manager.

In most cases, large companies or conglomerates produce many products—each of which has its own brand. Each of these brands is then treated like a mini business within the larger company. The brand manager is in charge of that mini-business and making sure that the brand is successful in the marketplace. Working alongside in-house departments as well as outside advertising and marketing agencies, and using creative marketing and advertising techniques, the brand manager begins building a favorable message or image about the product that she believes will resonate with potential customers. This usually involves testing the product (and its name) with targeted consumers; creating advertising and marketing campaigns which, in a few words,

CAREER 411

Search It!
The Association of Product Management at http://www.aipmm.com.

Surf It!
Go to http://www.instantshift.com/2009/01/29/20-corporate-brand-logo-evolution for a great look at 20 brands and how their logos evolved over the years.

Read It!
Go to http://www.inter-brand.com/en/knowledge.aspx for an interactive article on the best global brands.

Learn It!
Minimum Education: Bachelor's degree to get started. Master's preferred for advancement.

Typical Majors: Business administration, marketing, communications.

Special Skills: Clear written and verbal communication skills, decisive, strong analytical skills, excellent managerial skills, risk taker.

Earn It!
Median annual salary is $88,000.

(Source: http://www.allbusinessschools.com)

GET STARTED NOW!

- In School: English, accounting, and any courses related to marketing or media.
- After School: Get involved in a leadership role in one or more clubs (or start your own).
- Around Town: Pay attention to how businesses in your community attempt to win over customers. How many different ways can you find their "branding" at work?

convey that the product can be trusted; and ultimately, making sure that you're constantly distinguishing your product from the competition.

As a brand manager, you'll have to draw on a broad range of skills and abilities. You need to be able to analyze the potential buyers of the product and how to get those people to trust and buy your product instead of the competition's. Once you've created a vision you know will work, you have to first convince your bosses, and then all the departments within the larger company that will be working alongside you. After you've done all that, it's time to move from the big picture to the nitty-gritty details. That means making sure your plan is implemented correctly, on time, and within the established budget. You'll work with the marketing department to create promotions that will create your brand's image, hire and stay on top of the advertising agency, and more.

The Norbert Pip-Squeak series of cameras finally hits the market. You're done, right? Wrong! You're just beginning! You'll review and analyze sales reports to see if your vision is working.

IF YOU WERE. . .

As a brand manager for a popular soft drink product, how would you update the drink's image for an environmentally conscious young generation?

. . . MAKE IT REAL!

Choose your favorite soft drink brand. Start by researching the brand's past advertising campaigns and marketing style. Research and analyze the brand's main competition, and look for ways to stand out. Plot out ideas, slogans, and product spokespeople that would increase your brand's visibility, likability, trustworthiness, and green appeal.

You'll tweak the brand when necessary, go after new markets and potential customers, develop new advertising strategies, and move in new directions when the established direction isn't working anymore. A successful brand manager not only keeps up with changes in industry trends, but ends up creating those trends—an entrepreneurial spirit who stays in front of the competition while keeping one eye on the rearview mirror. All of this is done while moving forward with courage, flexibility, vision, and conviction.

Budget Analyst

Creating a budget for yourself means taking a look at the money you make, the bills you have to pay, and the stuff you need or want to buy, and making good decisions about how to allocate (or distribute) the money. A good budget sets aside money for short-term needs as well as for long-term goals, and it takes a certain level of responsibility to manage one's money well. Sometimes it means bypassing that new computer you want because you're saving for college or buying a used car instead of a brand-new one. A budget analyst helps make decisions like these all the time for companies, nonprofit organizations, and government agencies. They create, manage, study, oversee, and otherwise help make decisions about how the business spends its money.

Suppose you were the budget analyst for the school you currently attend. Think about the various things that need funding—salaries, facility upkeep, programs (sports, music, etc.), books, food. At the beginning of each budget cycle, you ask each department within your school or school district to create a budget for the upcoming year that includes a detailed list and explanation of its financial needs.

GET STARTED NOW!

- In School: Math, statistics, accounting, advanced computer courses, public speaking, economics, word processing, and spreadsheets.
- After School: Join or start a business club or debate club, and consider volunteering at a nonprofit organization.
- Around Town: Find out how local nonprofit organizations spend their money by reviewing annual reports and financial information from local nonprofit organizations (usually available online or upon request via a phone call).

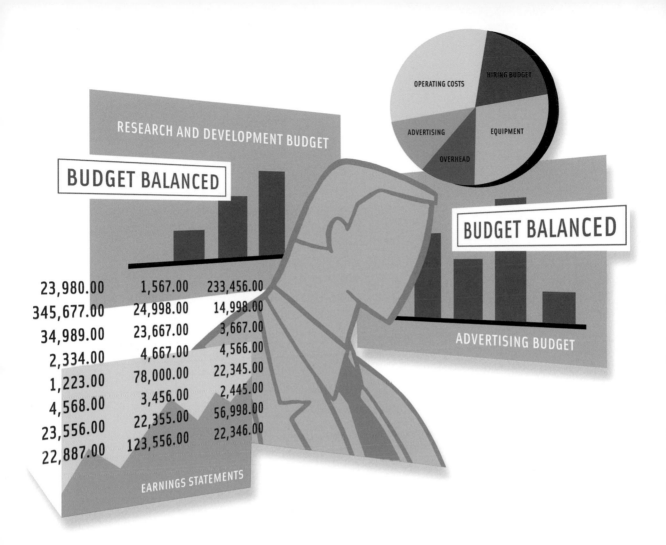

RESEARCH AND DEVELOPMENT BUDGET

BUDGET BALANCED

OPERATING COSTS

HIRING BUDGET

ADVERTISING

EQUIPMENT

OVERHEAD

BUDGET BALANCED

ADVERTISING BUDGET

23,980.00	1,567.00	233,456.00
345,677.00	24,998.00	14,998.00
34,989.00	23,667.00	3,667.00
2,334.00	4,667.00	4,566.00
1,223.00	78,000.00	22,345.00
4,568.00	3,456.00	2,445.00
23,556.00	22,355.00	56,998.00
22,887.00	123,556.00	22,346.00

EARNINGS STATEMENTS

You compile budgets and proposals from every department and examine them to make sure they're accurate and following the correct procedures. Once that's done, you review the numbers—weighing available monetary resources against budget requests—and begin figuring out how to allocate the organization's money appropriately and fairly. Once the evaluation of each department's budget is complete, you draft a suggested school budget—keeping the school's priorities and resources in mind. This process undoubtedly involves making cuts and compromises.

Then, it's time to work with the principal, the school superintendent, or others with final authority to turn the plan to an approved budget. Once the budget is approved and the resources are allocated, it's your job to monitor the budget by reviewing spending reports.

Whether working for a school district, a Fortune 500 corporation, or a philanthropic organization, the budget analyst must rely on his or her integrity and ethics to make tough decisions about budget cuts, program eliminations, and layoffs.

In order to do this job well, a budget analyst needs to be on top of local economic trends as well as potential financial developments that could affect how the organization spends its money. But even more than that, a successful budget analyst must know intimately how the organization operates. What do the employees absolutely need to get their jobs done? What are the consequences when you move money from one program to another one? That's why successful budget analysts suggest working for an organization that interests you. The more you care about the organization's products or mission, the more motivated you'll be to safeguard its assets.

Business Consultant

You've read your paper for English class over a dozen times and you think it's finally perfect; however, a friend takes one look at it and sees that you spelled Shakespeare wrong throughout and that you're missing a thesis statement. A business consultant is a lot like that friend, but instead of swooping in and helping one person, a business consultant is hired by a company to help them notice things that are not working and come up with solutions. Whereas you might actually resent your friend's constructive criticism (*there so is a thesis statement, doofus!*), companies pay good money for a business consultant's advice.

Companies experiencing rapid growth, seeking to maximize profits, or aiming to get on track in various areas of their business look to business consultants to streamline processes, increase productivity, work on digitizing part of the company's business, deal with human resources issues such as training and low employee morale, simplify communications, and more. Companies appreciate and are willing to pay for that outside point of view to locate glitches in systems that employees don't notice because they're too busy doing their jobs. Think of a business consultant as a salesperson, but instead of selling a product, you're selling innovative ideas that will ultimately help a company take steps for positive change.

As a business consultant, you'd most likely be working with a team that's put together by your firm to deal directly with the client's

CAREER 411

Search It!
Institute for Management Consultants USA at http://www.imcusa.org.

Surf It!
Go to http://www.vault.com for a list of the most prestigious consulting companies.

Read It!
Find out how business plans work at http://money.howstuffworks.com/business-plans.htm.

Learn It!
Minimum Education: Bachelor's degree.

Typical Majors: Business management, economics, marketing, finance.

Special Skills: Presentation skills, analytical, confident, self-motivated, good listener, curious, and business experience.

Earn It!
Median annual salary is $64,000.

(Source: http://www.payscale.com)

GET STARTED NOW!

- In School: Computer and business courses, writing, statistics, accounting, public speaking.
- After School: Consider tutoring students who need help in your best subjects.
- Around Town: Look for ways to improve the service you receive at local businesses.

needs. Each consultant in your team brings a certain expertise to the table, and as part of that team, they're relying on you to help get the job done. Each new assignment is unique and each of the complex problems you encounter will need creative thinkers and problem solvers who can work outside the box. You'll be assigned to work directly with the part of the company that's within your area of expertise. You'll watch how they do their jobs, communicate with your team members, and then begin putting together a comprehensive plan of action for the company. You'll rely on your acute listening and analytical skills as well as your ability to work alongside other experts (your colleagues), each of whom may have different ideas than you on how to "fix" your client.

Whether you're working with a client to help them launch a new product or to change the entire direction of a company, your success will be measured by how successful your clients are after your work is done. Did your fresh perspective affect positive change? Did the problems you helped solve stay solved? Has the client hired your firm for more business? Meanwhile, you've added yet more experience to your arsenal and are that much more prepared for the next assignment!

Business Development Director

TT Games is a British video game developer and publisher that has sold more than 45 million games. It has built its success through partnerships with blockbuster movies such as *Toy Story*, *The Chronicles of Narnia*, and more. In 2005, in a move that critics believed would never work, TT Games teamed up with LucasArts (of *Star Wars* fame) and Lego to create the first of its Lego video games: *Lego Star Wars: The Video Game*. The game, featuring the licensed *Star Wars* characters and scenes all in a Lego universe, beat all odds and became the 13th bestselling video game of the year. The concept of combining the two licenses took creativity, vision, salesmanship, and an ability to take risks—all the qualities needed in a business development director.

These days it's not enough for a company to rest on its laurels. In this increasingly competitive world, businesses must always stay informed of what their competitors are up to and they need to keep developing new and creative ways to expand their reach in the marketplace. (Partnering with other companies—like what TT Games did—is one example of this.) A company striving for new ideas, leads, and partnerships turns to its business development director.

CAREER 411

Search It!
Teen Business Forum at http://www.teenbusinessforum.com.

Surf It!
Play a business simulation game at http://www.tycoononline.nu.

Read It!
Read Marshall Brain's ideas about creativity in business at http://marshallbrain.com/million1.htm.

Learn It!
Minimum Education: Bachelor's degree or master's in business administration.

Typical Majors: Business, entrepreneurship, communications.

Special Skills: Excellent communication and negotiation skills, self-motivated, salesmanship.

Earn It!
Median annual salary is $103,000.

(Source: http://www.payscale.com)

GET STARTED NOW!

- In School: Public speaking, English, business, computers, accounting.
- After School: Debate club, Junior Achievement, or start your own business.
- Around Town: Visit online (or in person) the business development office or chamber of commerce in your area.

Known for being both an idea generator and a deal maker, the business development director identifies new business opportunities for the company, which can include new markets for existing products, partnerships with other companies, or even creating new products. Then the director must develop the plans with key staff within the company, sell them to chief executives, and finally bring these plans to fruition through keen negotiating skills. Other duties include keeping on top of the industry you're in, knowing where to invest the company's time and resources, creating long-term marketing strategies, and perhaps even suggesting smaller companies

to buy that will increase the organization's reach into an existing (or brand new) market. This job is all about seizing business opportunities and strategizing the best ways to forge a bright future for the organization.

You may start your career by cold-calling potential partners or clients or following up leads created by the director. This is the time for developing your people skills, your ability to sell and negotiate, as well as the self-confidence needed to pitch creative and risky business plans. And when you make it to the top and pitch, sell, and negotiate a deal like the Lego/*Star Wars* partnership, you will be congratulated—and in the next breath be asked, "What's next?" You are navigating the future of the company with the deals you make today, which makes for an exciting career for a creative, entrepreneurial risk taker.

Certified Public Accountant

Unless you're one of those teen entrepreneurial phenoms, it's pretty safe to say you can keep track of your money without any help. You know how much you get paid for the after-school job, and you're aware of any bills you need to pay every month. You can probably even take a fairly accurate guess at how much your assets are worth. As soon as any company, from a large corporation to a mom-and-pop shop, starts spending and making money, it needs to bring in the number crunchers—otherwise known as accountants. And, for several reasons, companies often prefer certified public accountants (known as CPAs) over accountants who don't have certification.

A public accountant usually works in an accounting firm, though some do have their own businesses. Corporations, smaller companies, nonprofit organizations, government agencies, and even individuals hire public accountants for several different accounting duties including ensuring that financial records are accurate; preparing tax returns and paying taxes on time; preparing and analyzing accounting records; examining business operations, trends, costs, and profits; studying financial data for signs of fraud or illegal activity; working on compensation and health care benefits; and helping with designing accounting systems.

GET STARTED NOW!

- In School: Math (including calculus) accounting, economics, computer classes.
- After School: Offer to be the treasurer for one or more clubs or teams, or consider running for class treasurer.
- Around Town: Interview CPAs and other public accountants in your area and ask what different functions they perform for clients.

If you work for yourself, you may find it more practical to be a generalist and offer most or all of these services. If you work for a firm, you will probably end up specializing in one of these areas. No matter which job you're performing for your client, you will be required to analyze spreadsheets and be a numbers detective—following the money trails to make sure it's all where it's supposed to be.

Anyone with a four-year college degree in accounting or finance can call themselves a public accountant and start working with clients. After working in the field for a while and making sure accounting is the career you wish to pursue, however, you should consider becoming licensed as a CPA. Being a CPA means that you have passed the Uniform Certified Public Accountant Examination (Uniform CPA Exam), which is set by the American Institute of Certified Public Accountants and given by the National Association of State Boards of Accountancy. In order to qualify for the test, you need up to 30 extra college credits (above and beyond the normal 120 you need for graduation) as well as a certain amount of work experience. (The actual requirements vary from state to state.)

It's a difficult test that takes a lot of preparation, but it's worth it. After receiving the CPA designation, not only will you make more money, but you can also provide more services for your clients. For instance, you can file a report with the Securities and Exchange Commission (SEC), as well as review and sign audit opinions, which are both important functions accountants are often called to perform. Being a CPA also gives your clients and your superiors a certain piece of mind and confidence that they have the right person for the job.

Chief Executive Officer

A publicly traded chain of bookstores suddenly finds profits plummeting after several years of increasing revenue. Foot traffic in all 700+ stores is down because of a recession; competition from online booksellers has cut into profits; and out of the blue, the digital revolution hits the industry, and people are buying e-books and e-readers. How does a company with this many stores and more than 30,000 employees shift gears quickly to meet the demands of this changing retail landscape? Ask the chief executive officer—the CEO.

Every business needs to have a focus and an overall strategy in order to get and remain successful. In most instances, responsibility for implementing the company's vision belongs to the person at the top: the chief executive officer. Steve Jobs, Jack Welch, and Bill Gates are just a few of the famous names that are or were chief executive officers. Most CEOs are not famous and don't make headlines, but their jobs are just as difficult and demanding as those in the limelight.

CEOs come from varied backgrounds and experiences. Some start their own businesses and are instant CEOs (e.g., Mark Zuckerberg, CEO of Facebook), while others have interesting stories about starting their careers in the mailroom and working their

CAREER 411

Search It!
The Chief Executive Officers' Clubs at http://www.ceoclubs.org.

Surf It!
Go to http://www.ceoonline.com.au/business_game.aspx to play "Who Wants to Be a CEO."

Read It!
Go to http://www.the-chiefexecutive.com for informative articles on CEOs, business solutions, and more.

Learn It!
Minimum Education: Bachelor's degree plus experience.

Typical Majors: Management, business administration, public administration, or liberal arts.

Special Skills: Strong leadership skills, administration and management, economics, accounting principles, knowledge of financial markets, strong presentation skills.

Earn It!
Median annual salary is $159,000.
(Source: U.S. Department of Labor)

GET STARTED NOW!

- In School: College preparation and AP courses, business, economics, advanced computer, accounting.
- After School: Seek out leadership positions in school clubs and join a local Junior Achievement program (http://www.ja.org).
- Around Town: Go to the library and find books on famous CEOs.

way to the top with determination, grit, smarts, and luck. And while CEOs make good money, it's a stressful position with long hours, a lot of travel, and intense pressure to keep being more profitable year after year.

As the highest-ranking person in the company, the CEO is in charge of the management of the organization, and must provide leadership in all facets of the running of company, even though they don't get involved too often with the day-to-day operations. Instead, they carry out strategic plans and policies that they created along with the organization's board of directors. CEOs plan how the company operates; assign leaders to ensure the company is following policies and overall strategies; and guide the perception of the company for employees, stockholders, and the general public. Other duties include advising the board on proper steps to take for future success, overseeing the design and introduction of new products and services, recommending the yearly budget for board approval, and managing the company's resources.

When everyone turns to the CEO of the bookstore chain for answers, the CEO is ready with a plan that takes on the online retailers, shifts the layout of the stores to make them more inviting for customers, and gives readers the books they want in whatever format they're looking for. And in order for it to be a good plan, it needs to take into account more than the CEO's short-term survival—it has to be a strategy that assures the long-term health and survival of the company itself.

Chief Financial Officer

A new automobile has just been released to the public, and the whole corporation is holding its collective breath to see how the new product will be received. After six months of sales, the board of directors and major shareholders want to know how the car is doing. The CEO is ready to release the number of cars sold because it's a good, strong number that will raise stock prices and keep the board off her back for a couple of months. But wait, the picture is a lot more complicated than that! The new cars are selling, but due to a factory strike and rising costs of materials, profit is low—too low to continue making the cars as is. It's not news the CEO wants to hear, but she trusts her source, the chief financial officer, and heads off to the board of directors meeting with the full, less rosy picture.

The chief financial officer (CFO) is the top dog when it comes to a company's financial matters. Whenever a business makes or spends money, the CFO's department knows about it, records it, and plans the next moves. This gives the CFO the information he needs to make the best recommendations to the CEO and the board. But reporting important and accurate financial information and acting as the key adviser on financial matters are only part of the CFO's duties.

If the corporation is seeking to buy or sell any of its assets such as other companies, the CFO is intricately involved. He also

GET STARTED NOW!

- In School: Calculus, AP courses, accounting, economics, statistics, computer classes.
- After School: Look into Junior Achievement (http://www.ja.org) and other business clubs.
- Around Town: Notice new businesses that pop up around town.

manages the corporation's other financial risks including how to invest its money and create the best balance between debt and equity. The CFO also manages all departments and divisions that deal with assets and liabilities. He reports on maximizing profits by controlling expenses, makes sure payroll is accurate and tax returns are properly filed, and creates financial controls and policies for the company. The CFO will also deal with banks and other financial institutions so the corporation can borrow money to fund future projects as well as develop good financial terms with vendors. And when it comes time to create the annual budget, it's the CFO's responsibility to make sure the budget will reflect the company's best interests and then report it to the CEO and board of directors.

A successful CFO doesn't simply present the bad news about automobile profits. He also works with engineers to lower the price of key components of the car, makes a deal with auto parts dealers for a new contract that promises them more business and lower prices for the corporation, and works with factory floor operators on creating a more efficient way to create the car. This plan saves the company millions and keeps the company in fantastic financial shape with its new, bestselling automobile for years to come.

Compensation and Benefits Manager

When you accept a job offer from a company, there's an implicit contract in effect: You will work for that company, and in return, it will pay you for your time and talents. As part of this contract, most companies also offer some sort of benefits package, which could include health insurance, life insurance, paid leave and vacation, 401(k) programs, pensions, and more. The human resources department handles all of these complicated matters, and the person in charge of making sense of it all for the company and its employees is the compensation and benefits manager.

As far as compensation is concerned, the compensation and benefits manager is responsible for establishing and maintaining the company's payroll system. This includes making sure the company is paying its employees competitively so it can attract the best talent out there. She must know all the duties and responsibilities of every job at the company, what competitors are paying people for these jobs, and the required skills needed to do the jobs.

GET STARTED NOW!

- In School: Speech, writing, communications, economics, accounting.
- After School: Volunteer your time at hospitals, assisted-living facilities, and homeless shelters—not only will you be helping others, but you'll also be developing your listening and communication skills.
- Around Town: Who pays your medical bills? Ask your parents to discuss how their places of employment assist with insurance and retirement.

CAREER 411

Search It!
Society for Human Resource Management at http://www.shrm.org.

Surf It!
Go to http://www.superhumanresourcescomic.com for a comic book series about a human resources department for superheroes!

Read It!
Go to http://www.howstuffworks.com/benefits.htm for good information on how benefits work.

Learn It!
Minimum Education: Bachelor's degree, with a master's degree to reach management positions.

Typical Majors: Business administration with an emphasis on human resources, human resources administration/management, psychology, public administration.

Special Skills: Empathy, good listening skills, accounting, business acumen, knowledge of labor laws, negotiation skills, discretion, analytic and research skills.

Earn It!
Median annual salary is $86,500.

(Source: U.S. Department of Labor)

And then she must balance all of that information to create a fair compensation for employees. Other responsibilities include determining when employees should be evaluated for possible raises and promotions, working with other departments on payroll budgets, and knowing the federal and state laws governing compensation and benefits.

The second part of the job entails analyzing, creating, and administering the employee benefits programs. It requires a breadth of knowledge of health and life insurance plans, disability programs, stock ownership plans, retirement programs, and more. The position also requires constant monitoring of these many programs—most of which are provided by outside companies. Can you negotiate lower fees from these companies? Are there better programs out there that need to be considered? Are these programs covering what the employees need? What are the alternatives, and can the company afford them? Other duties include creating sick- and paid-leave policies, finding and offering other employee perks such as discounts on gym memberships, and making sure employees understand the benefits they are receiving.

As a compensation and benefits manager, you must be a patient listener who's able to present information clearly and concisely. You're the person the employees come to, paycheck in hand, to ask for an explanation as to why their paycheck has changed or why they're suddenly contributing more toward their health insurance. Employees contact you when they have a sick family member and need an extended leave to care for them. And as the workforce changes, it's more important than ever to stay on top of new, innovative programs the company could offer, such as wellness programs, smoking cessation, lunchtime yoga, flexible hours, and more. Whereas in all other departments it's about increasing profits, yours is the one department where job satisfaction is expected to rise along with the profits.

Compliance Officer

CAREER 411

Search It!
The Ethics and Compliance Officer Association at http://www.theecoa.org and Society of Corporate Compliance and Ethics at http://www.corporatecompliance.org.

Surf It!
Go to http://www.compliance-officer.org for portals on different types of compliance businesses and a link to a free e-book called *100 Job Descriptions in Risk & Compliance Management*.

Read It!
Go to http://www.corporatecomplianceinsights.com/2010/evolving-role-of-chief-compliance-officer for a good article on how the chief compliance officer job is evolving.

Learn It!
Minimum Education: Bachelor's or master's degree.

Typical Majors: Business management, finance, accounting, economics, law.

Special Skills: Detail-oriented, excellent oral and written communication skills, inquisitive nature, respect for authority.

Earn It!
Median annual salary is $91,000.

(Source: http://www.salary.com)

From the plastic bag that warns parents not to let their children put it over their heads to the coffee cup that warns you that the contents inside are hot, everything these days has a warning label. These labels crop up due to lawsuits and then regulations set in place, usually by federal or state governments. It's a system that creates many, many regulations across all facets of industry, and though these are put in place to protect people, simply keeping on top of all the regulations is a full-time job.

The larger the corporation, and the more sensitive the industry, the more rules and regulations the organization will have to follow. There will be federal regulations, state regulations, local ordinances, industry guidelines, as well as internal company rules that all need to be adhered to. In smaller companies, human resource directors may be responsible for making sure all regulations are being followed; however, in large, heavily regulated industries such as health care, banking, and financial services, a compliance officer is hired to act as the super hall monitor for the organization.

The compliance officer must first know all the rules and laws that govern the industry his company is in. (This usually takes years of working within a specific industry.) There are guidelines

GET STARTED NOW!

- In School: English, writing, statistics, math, history.
- After School: Seek out ethics competitions (which are like debate team competitions) or writing contests, debate club.
- Around Town: Be on the lookout for unusual rules and try to surmise the thinking behind each one.

for building and worker safety—specifically the Occupational Health and Safety Administration Act (OSHA)—as well as for product safety, financial transactions, and ethical behavior. Next, the compliance officer must create (if not already done so) clear guidelines and procedures for each department in the company so that the rules can be followed easily. Then he implements the plans, trains the employees, and sets up a monitoring system to make sure everyone is compliant. He monitors not only for inadvertent breaches in protocol, but also for deliberate fraud and unethical behavior. The compliance officer also maintains the system for handling violations, responds to employees reporting alleged violations, keeps up with the ever-changing regulations, and answers any governing body outside the company wishing information.

Now while this job sounds like the hallway monitor at school, a successful compliance officer works within the different departments, providing sufficient support and training. He strives to create a sense of collaboration and cooperation as employees learn the internal and external regulations they need to incorporate into their daily workflow. If done well, instead of coming across as someone to hide from, employees seek out the compliance officer when they are confused or need help. He becomes someone the employees as well as upper management rely on to help them do their jobs in accordance to the many regulations they all have to follow. The compliance officer that creates an easy-to-follow system and remains independent and objective as he evaluates compliance will be considered effective and necessary for the company's continued success.

Corporate Communications Director

Apple has consistently rated in the top 10 of the "World's Most Admired Companies" (*Fortune* magazine) for several years and has been ranked number one for the past two years. How do they do it? Well, it doesn't hurt to provide products that redefine how people work, play, and live…but it's more than that. Apple doesn't just have customers; it has fans. And it takes a lot more than revolutionary products to create such positive brand awareness— it takes a strong and consistent message. From the charismatic CEO all the way down the corporate ladder to the Apple Store employee, Apple conveys confidence and a sense of superiority and trust. Consumers want to be part of the cutting edge, and they think Apple will give it to them. Whether or not this is true, people believe it. All companies want their name and brand to instill a positive message to its employees and the public, and they rely on corporate communications directors to make that happen.

As a company's corporate communications director, it's your job to craft this positive perception of your company—to implement, grow, maintain, and protect it during difficult situations.

GET STARTED NOW!

- In School: English, psychology, computer classes, creative writing, journalism, public speaking.
- After School: Yearbook (promoting a positive message about your high school!), debate team.
- Around Town: Keep a log of messages that are conveyed by different companies. See if you can hone each message down to one sentence. For example: Apple: We're reinventing your life.

This goes way beyond advertising and public relations and delves into message control. You must make sure everyone's on the same page and stays there. Any piece of information that emanates from your company (ads, brochures, blogs, TV commercials, speeches from executives, and more) needs to be scrutinized by your department to ensure it conveys the proper message about the company. You'll also create and maintain good relationships with the media, giving them the information they need while also maintaining a positive public image. You may draft speeches for the CEO, communicate the company's personality to employees, and create a crisis management plan. (Nothing sinks a company faster than an improperly handled scandal, product recall, or lawsuit.)

But this isn't a job about lying. Sure, you're crafting a message, but in the best of situations the message you're promoting is based on quality products and an ethical, conscientious company. You can't force employees to feel proud of where they work. The only way to convey a positive message to employees is to create a dynamic workplace where they are listened to, the product they're

IF YOU WERE. . .

As a corporate communications director in charge of explaining an accidental mishap involving significant environmental consequences (think BP oil spill in 2010), how would you inform the world?

. . . MAKE IT REAL!

Research corporate mess-ups such as the BP oil spill, Toyota's gas pedal recall, and the Carnival "Spam" cruise. Use lessons learned from these classic public relations nightmares to write a press release, CEO speech, or TV ad that addresses the problem in a way you think will preserve the company's positive persona. Choose a recent example from the news or create your own scenario.

working on is good, and the company cares for them. It's your job to work with top executives to make that happen. As for the public, they won't be fooled for long by empty promises and shoddy workmanship. You must help create a strong work culture where the company's vision and values are put into action every day. Take care of these factors and the message becomes very easy to promote. The employees, consumers, stockholders, bloggers, and others will do your work for you.

CAREER 411

Search It!

Visit BSR (a network of sustainable businesses) at http://www.bsr.org or Global Reporting Initiative at http://www.globalreporting.org.

Surf It!

Go to http://3blmedia.com/theCSRminute for a daily video digest of CSR trends, topics, and breaking news.

Read It!

Search *Business Respect* magazine (http://www.businessrespect.net) for an online journal featuring stories of businesses and their successes (or lack thereof) in social responsibility.

Learn It!

Minimum Education: Master's degree.

Typical Majors: Corporate responsibility, business, economics, environmental studies.

Special Skills: Strong written and verbal communication skills, ability to multitask, strong ethics and integrity, good public relations skills, strong research skills.

Earn It!

Median annual salary is $90,000.

(Source: http://www.salary.com)

Corporate Social Responsibility Manager

You always recycle, buy organic, and treat others with respect because you are a responsible member of your community. Many companies have realized that they must act as responsible global community members, too. That means taking into account how their businesses affect people and the planet. Starbucks is a good example; they annually rank as one of the most socially responsible companies. Along with their profit goals, they set goals for community service, sustainable practices, and ethical coffee purchases. They even offer balanced food and beverage options to customers. Many corporations have begun to rely on corporate social responsibility managers to help set, manage, and promote socially and environmentally friendly policies.

Policies that affect internal company operating procedures could govern standardized handling of hazardous materials, company recycling programs, and corporate giving to charities. Internal policies can also set the tone for how a corporation treats its workers, and may include diversity training or programs that emphasize valuing employees. External policies, on the other hand, deal with the company's effect on the outside world. Such

GET STARTED NOW!

- In School: Environmental studies, business, marketing classes, sociology.
- After School: Volunteer for local environmental groups or for a business with a triple bottom line (people, planet, profit).
- Around Town: Support local companies that take a socially responsible stance or are working toward a triple bottom line.

policies might require corporations to choose suppliers that use environmentally friendly methods, apply fair trade practices when harvesting natural resources or crops, and govern proper waste disposal. A socially responsible corporation would not illegally mine granite, dump chemicals in rivers, ignore child labor laws, or contract with a sweatshop.

Once socially responsible policies have been agreed upon, corporate social responsibility managers must implement procedures for following those policies. They monitor how well the company adheres to the policies, and meet with company stakeholders (shareholders, board members, executives, and customers) to explain and enforce them. A corporate social responsibility manager may also work with charity partners to plan events and publicize donations.

There is often a price to be paid for corporate social responsibility, and it's usually in decreased profits. It can be more expensive to use hardwood or coffee or stone that is ethically harvested. Utilizing suppliers who pay employees fair wages can also mean higher cost. For this reason, many criticize an overemphasis on corporate social responsibility as taking away from the true goal of business, which is to make money. It is the corporate social responsibility manager's task to help executives and shareholders weigh costs against the benefits in order to make balanced decisions. Fortunately, corporations can offset some costs. Social responsibility is great public relations. People like supporting companies they feel good about, and socially responsible companies are popular with talented, young recruits who want to work for a company that does good in the world and that takes a longer view of profitability. Under the guidance of a competent corporate social responsibility manager, a corporation that successfully embraces a socially responsible philosophy will be able to grab profits and embrace accountability at the same time.

Corporate Trainer

Imagine you're starting a new after-school job at a fast food restaurant. On your first day, you're led to the kitchen area, given an apron and a paper hat, and told to make some fries. Even if you've made fries at home, you have no idea how to work the fryer. Now imagine someone finally helps you out that first day and you get the hang of the fryer, only to come to work a week later and find a brand new fryer that *no one* knows how to use. Orders lay there unfilled, customers begin to complain, and chaos ensues. This is what life would be like at large companies without corporate trainers.

Rapidly changing technology, complex rules and regulations, and new information and job duties can overwhelm even seasoned, competent workers—resulting in a decrease in productivity and employee frustration. This lack of knowledge ultimately keeps the employees and the company from reaching their full potential. Corporate trainers, either from within the company or from an outside firm, are brought in to teach the new skills and information to departments that need them. So, whether an employee is starting the first day of work at the company, is preparing for a new position that requires greater skill, or simply needs help doing their job right now, the corporate trainer creates, schedules, and implements the program necessary to get that employee up to speed quickly.

GET STARTED NOW!

- In School: Public speaking or speech classes, psychology.
- After School: Join or start a peer-tutoring program, drama club.
- Around Town: Offer to mentor or tutor younger students in a subject you're particularly strong in.

CAREER 411

Search It!
The American Society for Training & Development at http://www.astd.org.

Surf It!
Go to http://www.corporategames.com to read about a company that provides a variety of creative corporate training options.

Read It!
Go to http://www.hrmreport.com/article/Top-trends-in-e-learning-and-corporate-training for an interesting article on e-learning.

Learn It!
Minimum Education: Bachelor's degree.

Typical Majors: Communications, human resources, psychology, education, social sciences.

Special Skills: Adept at teaching and public speaking, strong team-building skills, good communication and organizational skills.

Earn It!
Median annual salary is $55,000.

(Source: http://www.mypursuit.com)

Some of the types of "lessons" corporate trainers create include on-the-job training for new employees, effective negotiation strategies for employees working with vendors, interpersonal skills for managers needing help dealing effectively with staff, leadership development for employees wishing to move up in the organization, policy changes, public speaking, team building, new technology how-to, and more. From helping customer service representatives improve their phone skills to teaching supervisors how to keep morale high during the busy season, each program designed by the corporate trainer has two goals: to make employees more effective at their jobs and increase company profits.

Corporate trainers need to be master teachers to succeed at their jobs. They need to be dynamic performers who know how to hold the attention of a group of people who, quite frankly, may not wish to be there. They also need to engage the trainees with a variety of teaching strategies to make sure what they need to learn sticks. These strategies can include hands-on activities, group games, slide presentations, job swaps, interactive online courses, videos, and more. The successful corporate trainer also keeps on

IF YOU WERE. . .

As a corporate trainer for a company specializing in training teachers to use social media tools in the classroom, what teaching techniques would you utilize in your training?

. . . MAKE IT REAL!

Think of the teachers you've learned from throughout the years. List the qualities of the teachers you believe you've learned the most from. Interview teachers at your school and ask them what they believe makes a teacher excel. Finally, create a corporate trainer guidebook with tips, tricks, and techniques from master teachers.

top of new insights into how people retain information and learns from past training sessions so that each new class is better than the one before it. With the swift pace of change in all industries, the corporate trainer's job has become even more essential for a healthy, thriving company, where the most valued asset of that company is its employees.

Customer Service Representative

The next time you have to call a credit-card company or your cell-phone service provider, try to get past the computerized options and talk with a live person. How long are you kept on hold? When you get someone, how does he greet you? Are you met with a friendly sounding person who wants to help you, or do you get the feeling he would rather be doing *anything else* than be on the phone with you? Even though you're talking to one person, how he interacts with you affects how you feel about the whole company. This critical "voice" of the company is the customer service representative—the primary way large companies interact with their customers.

"How may I help you?" It's a polite question that you will ask countless times a day as a customer service representative. It's also an important one because, as the first line of contact for the customers, it's your job to make sure they come away from their time with you with the correct answers to their questions and a feeling that they just had a positive encounter. Most large companies rely

GET STARTED NOW!

- In School: Computer classes, English, business classes, sociology, public speaking.
- After School: Join the debate club, familiarize yourself with computer database programs, or volunteer to answer phones for nonprofit organizations that need help.
- Around Town: Get a part-time job in retail or in another industry where you will be required to assist customers.

on pools of customer service representatives to answer phone calls and e-mails, as well as to handle online customer service operations, and each interaction is an opportunity to retain a customer or gain a new one. Hence, manners, pleasant demeanor (even under stress), and a true ability to provide help are all important traits for the customer service representative.

On the surface, it may seem like an easy job: you answer questions and resolve complaints. And while many of the requests will be relatively simple to deal with (What's my balance? When's my bill due? How do I update my online profile?), there will be plenty of challenges during the day. From aggressive, angry, and rude customers and complicated situations that require help from your supervisor and/or other departments, to the sometimes repetitive nature of the job and the quota of calls you need to take per shift, you're constantly multitasking and rushing—all with a "smile" in your voice.

What kinds of calls you answer depends on the industry. If you work at a bank, for instance, you'll work with customers on their account questions. If you work for a major retailer, you may take orders, deal with returns, or help customers navigate the company's Web site. In each instance, you'll follow strict company guidelines when dealing with customers. You'll also be closely monitored, so that if you end up being one of those representatives who sounds like he'd rather be anywhere else, you probably *will* be somewhere else, and without a job. Meanwhile, since this is an entry-level position for most companies, if you leave even your most irate customers satisfied, you and your professional manner will soon find your way up the corporate ladder.

Dispatcher

Two calls came in overnight. A tree fell on Maple Street and Mrs. Blankenship's cable is out. Dr. Farnsworth on Highway 31 is having televisions installed in his dental office and needs hookup ASAP. You, the dispatcher, pull up Wednesday's schedule. You already have service trucks on Highway 31, so you call in Dr. Farnsworth's service. Maple Street is no problem if Mrs. Blankenship can be there in the morning; you have a truck nearby at 10:30. You log in the calls, schedule the appointments, and answer the ringing phone.

"Dispatch" means "send away." A dispatcher sends people or equipment to work. This work can include services like cable installation, but it can also include scheduling truckers to haul freight, or dispatching vehicles to carry passengers or deliver cargo. It can mean sending ambulances and fire trucks to answer calls, or scheduling work crews to handle maintenance. Many services, like cleaning and lawn care, are completed for customers regularly. A dispatcher also handles extra work. If it isn't time for Mr. Goble's quarterly lawn service but he wants to spruce up the yard for a party, a dispatcher would send a crew to handle the extra service.

Dispatchers use computers, two-way radios, or cell phones to contact workers. A dispatcher may also check to make sure

GET STARTED NOW!

- In School: English, public speaking, and logic.
- After School: Work on a schedule for your activities. On a calendar, write in the activities you have regularly. In a different color, add in extra activities as they pop up.
- Around Town: Ask your family to let you plan the route for Saturday errands.

SHIPPING SCHEDULE

that service was received at the appointed time. (There is usually a window of time. Workers rarely know exactly how long jobs will take.) An unreliable or slow worker reflects badly on the company and can mean angry calls about no-shows or jobs poorly done.

Heavy equipment takes great effort to move around, so a heavy equipment dispatcher must know a lot of detail about potential jobs. For example, if a land clearing business's dispatcher sends bulldozers and dump trucks to sites, the dispatcher needs to know exactly what equipment is needed. Sending too little or too much equipment is a costly mistake.

Transportation dispatchers have a challenging job. Many truckers follow regular routes, but dispatchers must juggle the exceptions with the regular jobs to save the company's money and the drivers' time. For example, if a dispatcher sends a trucker from Orlando, Florida, to Little Rock, Arkansas, with a load of freight, he must find freight in Little Rock to go to another destination, because an empty truck makes for a wasted trip. A dispatcher must also reroute drivers around roadwork, accidents, and bad weather. Companies that receive late freight deliveries will charge penalties or switch suppliers.

Being a dispatcher means being organized and having a thick skin. When scheduling others' time on behalf of a business, if things do not happen as planned, workers and customers get frustrated. An efficient dispatcher handles problems effectively, but tries hard to prevent problems in the first place.

E-Commerce Analyst

CAREER 411

Search It!
Click here for a list of Web analytics terms: http://www.webtrends.com/Education/Glossary.aspx.

Surf It!
Try the E-Commerce Times at http://www.ecommercetimes.com/?wlc=1285439866 to keep up-to-date on selling and marketing on the Internet.

Read It!
Read about the history of e-commerce at http://communication.howstuffworks.com/history-e-commerce.htm.

Learn It!
Minimum Education: Bachelor's degree.

Typical Majors: Communications, marketing, computer, statistics, Web site design.

Special Skills: Excellent analytical and organizational skills, ability to work well under pressure and handle stress, excellent computer and communication skills, time management skills, and ability to meet deadlines.

Earn It!
Median annual salary is $77,010.

(Source: U.S. Department of Labor)

First, you check the Web site's page-visit count. It's up 150 percent from this same time last week, and online sales are up 6 percent. The site's new design and newly implemented search engine optimization plan have turned into dollars. Your marketing supervisor is happy. Your next task is to research viral marketing possibilities. You will also ask your Webmaster to add new keywords to the Web site. Last, you write up the terms of your next e-mail promotion idea.

Many businesses market and sell goods and services online. Companies employ e-commerce analysts to increase sales through online channels. It is the analyst's job to know the latest e-commerce trends. For example, viral marketing—passing advertising information through word of mouth—is popular right now, as is advertising on social media sites. The e-commerce analyst decides how to best to utilize those channels to sell more goods and services. An e-commerce analyst also looks at company placement on search engine lists, looks for smart sites on which to place paid ads, and is constantly striving to increase online market share.

GET STARTED NOW!

- In School: Computer classes, business and marketing.
- After School: Familiarize yourself with computer Web analysis programs like http://www.google.com/analytics.
- Around Town: Visit a local store that has a Web site, such as a local kids' hangout that lets parents schedule birthday parties online. Interview the store manager or owner and find out how effectively their Web site increases traffic for their business.

For example, a company that sells concert tickets would need to make sure that it appears near the top on searches for the word "tickets" plus keywords for popular bands, sports teams, and other events. The ticket company could use viral marketing of live concert footage, or send out e-mail offers for a chance to win backstage passes if you buy tickets online. The e-commerce analyst makes sure all of this happens.

Being an e-commerce analyst is not just about the latest trends. E-commerce analysts have to show results. They constantly must ask and answer questions like: Does the Web site reach our goal for visits per day? How long does the average online visitor stay on our site? How do we know a viral marketing campaign will increase our sales? What new e-commerce marketing opportunities are out there? Does our online store sell products efficiently? Does the site encourage add-on sales?

In other words, for every e-commerce marketing or sales idea, there must be figures that justify spending the time and money. E-commerce analysts must be able to prove that redesigning the Web site or changing the online sales processes results in more sales. This can be hard to do, and an analyst must gather and use data about Web traffic and compare sales figures to decide which online marketing plans and purchasing procedures are effective. By staying current about trends, and by thinking critically about data and online initiatives, a good e-commerce analyst will make the most of every "e-opportunity."

Entrepreneur

At age 13, Sean Belnick enjoyed selling Pokémon cards over the Internet. This passion for online commerce led him to set up a small business selling office chairs. By age 18, Sean was a millionaire. There are hundreds of stories of teens striking it rich by starting their own businesses (many of them online), and if you have a passion for something (as well as persistence), you may already be on your way. You don't have to wait to be a certain age or have a particular college degree to start your own business—you just need to have the head and heart of an entrepreneur.

Nearly every business out there was, at one point, the germ of an idea that turned into a plan which one or more entrepreneurial spirits decided to put into action. Instead of confining themselves to an office and a set routine, they struck out on their own to create their fortune. Entrepreneurs share several common traits: They're independent, driven, quick-learning, nontraditional thinkers who aren't afraid to make mistakes and quite often jump in first and ask questions later. And they like making money! Most entrepreneurs have good business sense and know how to manage their time well. And while they do much of the work getting their business off the ground, the most successful entrepreneurs know that they can't do everything by themselves and must hire others to fill specific roles.

GET STARTED NOW!

- In School: Accounting, business, computer classes, math, English.
- After School: Start your own business or join Junior Achievement (http://www.ja.org).
- Around Town: Research teen entrepreneurs online.

CAREER 411

Search It!
Visit the Entrepreneurs' Organization at http://www.eonetwork.org and Collegiate Entrepreneurs' Organization at http://www.c-e-o.org.

Surf It!
Go to http://www.simunomics.com for a fun, online game where you're the boss of a brand new company and it's your job to make a fortune!

Read It!
Find resources for young entrepreneurs at http://www.sbaonline.sba.gov/teens/ and http://www.youngentrepreneur.com.

Learn It!
Minimum Education:
None, but an associate's or bachelor's degrees is helpful.

Typical Majors: Entrepreneurship, business, finance, marketing.

Special Skills: Self-motivated, self-disciplined, risk taker, creative, focused.

Earn It!
Median annual salary varies according to the business.

It's difficult to nail down the exact job duties of an entrepreneur; however, once the product is developed or the Web site is created, entrepreneurs wear several hats. They need to market their product, hire freelancers or employees, and then act as a human resources department, keep close track of the money coming in and the money going out, and more. In other words, entrepreneurs are the CEOs, CFOs, CPAs, IT managers, and then some!

One of the keys to being a successful entrepreneur is doing something you're passionate about. If you have a particular skill or hobby, see if you can turn it into a business. For example, if you love art and graphic design, start your own Web site design business. If you love collecting autographs of your favorite sports stars, open your own online sports memorabilia store. Or, look at industries that are ripe for innovation. Green entrepreneurs are creating new, environmentally friendly products and are also consulting with homeowners and businesses on how they can lower their carbon footprint. Meanwhile the Internet is a veritable breeding ground for entrepreneurs—especially for teens.

Being an entrepreneur is not for everyone. There can be a lot of risk involved, and depending on your business, you may have to lay out a large chunk of your own money to get started. And don't expect anyone to invest in your company until you have customers and revenue. But if the idea of creating something on your own and working hard to make it succeed appeals to you, it may actually be difficult to think of working for someone else's bright idea.

Facilities Manager

CAREER 411

Search It!

International Facilities Management Association at http://www.ifma.org.

Surf It!

Go to http://www. todaysfacilitymanager.com and http://www.fmlink.com for facility management news and trends.

Read It!

Imagine what it would be like to manage an international airport at http://www. howstuffworks.com/transport/flight/ modern/airport.htm.

Learn It!

Minimum Education: Bachelor's degree.

Typical Majors: Engineering, architecture, construction management, business administration, or facility management.

Special Skills: An interest in architecture and/or engineering, management skills, strong communication skills, multitasking.

Earn It!

Median annual salary is $73,500.

(Source: U.S. Department of Labor)

Imagine what your home would look like if no one did their chores for a couple of weeks: dishes and garbage piled up everywhere, broken appliances sitting there useless, and dirt and dust everywhere. It's not an efficient or sanitary way to live, which is why parents insist that chores get done. Now, even though smart phones, the Internet, and laptop computers have freed traditional white-collar employees to work wherever they want, most still report to an office building every day. And when they walk through the doors each morning, they expect the elevator to work, the offices to be clean, and the temperature to be just right. Unlike home, however, there is someone who takes on all the building responsibilities so employees can concentrate on their jobs instead of cleaning the bathrooms each morning before checking their e-mail.

This "super mom" is the facilities manager, and before you get the wrong idea with the analogy above, the job is much more than making sure the building is clean. In fact, this position requires specialized effort and know-how, as most large companies rely on a facilities manager to choreograph the myriad details involved in keeping a building ready for business every single day.

Facilities managers don't create the products or perform the services their companies offer to consumers, but they make sure employees have a safe and comfortable environment in which to work. One part of the job does entail managing the main-

GET STARTED NOW!

- In School: English composition, physics, math, and any course relating to design or architecture.
- After School: Volunteer for Habitat for Humanity projects (http://www.habitat.org).
- Around Town: Look for ways to do your chores more efficiently.

tenance staff: making
sure waste is properly dis-
posed of, facilities are sanitary, and
the grounds surrounding the building are
neat and clean. Another part of the job involves space management, from making sure new employees have appropriate places to
work and moving departments when necessary to making sure the
air quality is good and the temperature is appropriate. The facilities manager also makes sure the building is up to code as far as
safety and security are concerned and that the building meets all
environmental regulations. They also plan, design, and supervise
building renovations, manage lease agreements with other tenants
of the building (if the company owns the building), supervise the
maintenance staff, and negotiate and hire repair contractors.

Facilities managers will either work directly for the company
or may be part of a management consulting firm that's hired on
a contractual basis. Along with buildings belonging to corporations, facilities managers may also work for apartment complexes,
sports stadiums, hospitals, convention centers, schools, hotels,
and shopping malls. A good facilities manager needs to be a well-
organized and disciplined overseer of the building and of the staff

that he manages. Knowledge of construction, zoning restrictions, and accounting are also highly regarded in this position. How do you know if you're doing a good job? If employees forget you exist because the building has become an ideal environment in which to work!

Human Resources Director

When a company gets ready to launch a new product or service, many things need to happen: The product needs to be designed and manufactured, marketing and advertising departments have to begin promoting the product, and sales personnel have to be trained to sell the product. This usually means it's time to hire new employees. And if the company wants the product to be of superior quality and to be able to compete in the marketplace, it will want to hire the best possible employees available. Department managers don't have the time or the training to take on this daunting task, which is why companies have a department dedicated to recruiting and hiring the best new employees and implementing strategies to keep new and existing employees working for the company. The human resources department is a beehive of activity that doesn't sell, market, or otherwise involve themselves in the company's products, but instead is responsible for the company's most valuable assets: its employees.

The human resources (HR) director manages the day-to-day administrative operations of the human resources department, which includes: providing training and career development; maintaining and improving working conditions; paying employees; creating, implementing, and explaining benefits and retirement plans; recruiting and interviewing potential employees for

CAREER 411

Search It!
Society for Human Resource Management at http://www.shrm.org and National Human Resources Association at http://www.humanresources.org.

Surf It!
Go to http://www.hr.com/neweconomy and http://www.hr.com/grow for humorous videos that look at the challenges many HR professionals face.

Read It!
Go to http://www.workforce.com for *Workforce Management* magazine.

Learn It!
Minimum Education: Bachelor's or master's degree.

Typical Majors: Human resources administration and management, public administration.

Special Skills: Excellent communication skills, creative thinker, good negotiation skills, knowledge of labor laws, good customer service skills, knowledge of business and management principles.

Earn It!
Median annual salary is $96,000.
(Source: U.S. Department of Labor)

GET STARTED NOW!

- In School: English, writing, speech, computer classes, psychology, economics.
- After School: Join a Junior Achievement program and volunteer as a peer mentor.
- Around Town: Look into job shadowing a human resources employee or find a human resources director of a local company and interview him.

job vacancies; terminating employment and administering other disciplinary procedures; creating policies (sexual harassment and equal opportunity, for example); advising managers on conducting themselves properly when dealing with subordinates, and more.

The best HR departments are trusted places where an employee can go to gripe, file a formal complaint against another employee, ask for help with a superior, request further job training, or where two employees can go to attempt a conflict resolution. It's also the place to go for information on what your options are if you need extended time off to deal with a sick family member, what your health insurance covers, how to best utilize the company's retirement plan, and what to do if you're injured on the job. The director makes sure that the department is following all company policies as well as all the government's rules and regulations regarding employee care, and that all the information they receive about the company's employees remains confidential.

But the human resources director's job goes beyond managing these myriad tasks. Successful management of a company's employees includes having a complete understanding of the busi-

IF YOU WERE. . .

As a human resources director, what strategies would you utilize to increase job satisfaction?

. . . MAKE IT REAL!

Think of all the perks, such as employee discounts, flex scheduling, and more that you could offer. Create a fun human resources board game that pits human resources directors against an office maze of perks, missed opportunities, and more. (For example: You implement a job advancement program, move ahead six spaces. You switch benefits providers to a cheaper one that offers less to employees, lose a turn.)

ness the company is running, what the employees' needs are, what the current mood is of the employees, and then creating a strategic, company-wide plan for increasing job satisfaction. The director collaborates with top executives to create polices that will limit job turnover (which has more to do with job satisfaction than simply giving out raises!), increasing job efficiency, and, in short, improving results of individuals, departments, and the whole company.

Importer/Exporter

Importing and exporting are two sides of the same coin. That coin is the process of selling goods in one country to people in another. This job market should expand with the growing global economy. People who are fascinated by travel and other cultures can often turn that enthusiasm into an exciting and fulfilling career in importing and exporting.

To become an importer/exporter, you must spot a demand for something that cannot easily be harvested, mined, or manufactured in some places. For example, say that you live in Honduras, and you know that the locals love maple syrup but cannot find it in stores. Further research shows there is a market for it. A quick Internet search turns up a host of American and Canadian maple syrup farmers who want to export their syrup. (You can also contact an export trading company (ETC) to find manufacturers to export goods.) You contact several maple farms and find two that are interested in exporting to Honduras. You now negotiate pricing, which includes paying farmers for the syrup, paying shipping and customs fees, and probably hiring a freight forwarder (someone who knows shipping costs and routes, and books space on ships or trucks to move the

GET STARTED NOW!

- In School: Marketing, business, economics, foreign language, and geography.
- After School: Go through your house and make a list of all the different countries where products you own have come from.
- Around Town: Visit a local store that carries imported goods—specialty foods, furniture, and electronics are safe bets. Compare pricing and quality between imported goods and locally made goods.

syrup). Add your fees for brokering the deal and tack on shipping insurance costs, and you can quote the price to Honduran distributors.

As an exporter, consider the same scenario—except now, you live in Vermont. Your honest, reliable neighbors make fabulous maple syrup. Your research says that syrup is sought after and hard to find in Honduras. You could contact an export management company (EMC) to find distributors and do other legwork like packaging, marketing, and arranging shipping. Or, you can search for distributors yourself. If you make contacts, you will present a price package to distributors that includes the cost of the syrup; shipping costs, arrangements, and insurance; and your fees. You may work with a manufacturer's representative that specializes in exporting food products. You will also need information about potential retailers in order to make sure the distributor

IF YOU WERE...

As an importer looking to import chocolate for gourmet markets, where (as in what countries) would you be most likely to find the basic raw material (cocoa) for importing?

...MAKE IT REAL!

Use the Internet to find at least three places in the world where cocoa flourishes. Find out all you can about each source using resources like the CIA's *World Factbook* (https://www.cia.gov/library/publications/the-world-factbook). Create a compare-and-contrast chart listing the pros and cons of working with each country.

has a market. Once you have signed contracts on both ends, you can start moving syrup.

Importers and exporters must be prepared to track shipments, deal with customs regulations, negotiate contracts, and trouble-shoot any problems with the supply end, the demand end, at customs, or during transport.

Importers and exporters count on traveling to meet with supply and demand contacts. Importing and exporting requires a lot of time and attention, but the payoffs can be huge—especially if you live in Honduras and crave maple syrup.

Information Technology Manager

Computers need a lot of TLC. Software needs updating, hard drives have to be replaced, networks must be established, and then there's overseeing the Internet connection and making sure e-mail works, addressing viruses, spam, crashes, data loss, and so on. If it feels like a full-time job taking care of one computer, imagine taking care of 50, 500, or even 1,000 computers (as well as dealing with the 50, 500, or even 1,000 employees using those computers). Well, it's no sweat for the information technology (IT, for short) manager. In fact, he is just as comfortable lying under a desk with a handful of cables in one hand and a phone in the other as he is at patiently working with employees on their computer problems. And that's just one of the many exciting aspects of this career.

So, beyond telling employees to hit Ctrl-Alt-Delete and basically acting as a weird sort of guidance counselor for the often complex relationship between computers and their humans, the IT manager also coordinates, plans, directs, and designs all the computer- and electronic-network-related activities of the company. Job duties vary depending on the size of the company, but in the larger organizations, the IT manager can add supervising

GET STARTED NOW!

- In School: Math, business, Web site design, computer science, calculus.
- After School: Volunteer at the school's computer lab and offer to set up friends' and family members' computers.
- Around Town: Stay up-to-date on the latest technology with frequent visits to the places that sell them.

a team of IT experts (software engineers, programmers, system analysts, and support specialists) to his list of duties as well as overseeing the telephone systems. In other words, information is king, and the IT manager is in charge of making sure it all gets where it needs to go quickly and safely.

Most companies link the employees' computers to one or more networks where information can be accessed and stored. The IT manager maintains these networks, providing the upkeep and security needed. This involves testing the networks for programming glitches that could cause a network to go down as well as creating new networks as needed. IT managers also have to keep on top of the latest technology and continually assess when the company should update software, hardware, and computers. Many companies also have the IT department monitor employees' usage of Internet, e-mail, and the networks. They provide training materials and classes to employees, work to prevent data loss, manage backup systems, purchase what the company needs, and in some cases oversee Web development and intranet sites.

Since IT is a central component of any organization, your decisions and strategies as an IT manager will directly affect the company's profitability and workers' abilities to do their jobs. You will not only help determine the organization's goals in this area, but executives will look to you for leadership—especially since most of the time you will know way more about the technology than they will. It's up to the IT manager to keep the company on the cutting edge of communication and information sharing, storage, and security.

International Business Consultant

It can be very complicated to successfully own and manage a business in another country. International corporations must know all about rules and regulations, customs, markets, and competitors in all of the countries where they have expanded or hope to expand. Enter the international business consultant. An international business manager can provide that information, and can help ease the opening or smooth the operation of the business.

Previous experience living or working abroad is a great asset, as is previous experience in international business or management. Some consultants remain in the United States and maintain contact with various international partners. Other consultants actually live and work abroad. In any case, travel is necessary to make new contacts abroad and to research markets, acquisition prospects, and potential business partners—and monitor competitors.

For example, if you are an international business consultant, and you have a client or work for a corporation that manufactures MP3 players, you might travel to India to research distributors, examine sales figures, and talk with electronics store managers about how well your sales stack up against domestic brands. Next you might travel to Slovenia to meet with a potential new busi-

GET STARTED NOW!

- In School: Business, foreign languages, world geography, international studies.
- After School: Join the Spanish, French, German, or other language club to learn more about customs in countries that speak that language.
- Around Town: Explore (and taste!) different kinds of international cuisine in your town.

ness partner who wants to import and distribute your client's MP3 players. You will spend the evening after your business dinner preparing a report for your client that explains the possible opportunities for partnering with the Slovenian company. Later you will tour their distribution and retail centers.

The next day you will spend some additional time talking to customs agents, visiting the U.S. embassy, and reading news of Slovenia's political climate in order to help your client anticipate any pitfalls in doing business with this country. After composing your second report, it is on to Mexico to follow up with some MP3 factories that want advice on passing through customs more easily. As you navigate through each country, you make sure to brush up on local culture and languages, relying on interpreters when necessary. You are careful not to offend your hosts by being very aware of and attentive to their beliefs and customs.

International business consultants can work for one corporation or many. They can have exciting jobs and may travel a lot. Because of the travel and the urgency of the information that is needed, long hours are normal for this job. But the adventure can certainly make up for it. Hey, you can always sleep on the plane!

Logistics Planner

It's back to school time! Actually it's always back to school time at your company. Your company owns factories that manufacture notebooks, pencils, notebook paper, and erasers. It's your job to create the annual logistics plan for providing an increased volume of goods to fill the backpacks of students everywhere just when they need them most—the beginning of a new school year.

Logistics planning is a very broad job category, but essentially it means coordinating and planning the details of a business, especially when it comes to the supply chain. A logistics planner might source raw materials, plan for warehouse space, analyze delivery routes and schedules, or work with suppliers to receive parts or finished goods. A good logistics planner achieves optimum efficiency at a minimal price. Logistics managers work with warehouse managers, dispatchers, distributors, and purchasing managers to achieve this goal.

To meet back-to-school demand, you might start at the end of the cycle—the date when retail stores expect your product to be in their warehouses and on their shelves. Next you talk with each factory's production manager to find out when the additional inventory will be available. You give these dates to all four warehouse managers, so that they can begin preparing warehouse space. Just before production begins, you work with the purchasing manager to source additional wood pulp for your paper needs. You are using a new company, and you successfully negotiate getting the pulp at a lower cost.

GET STARTED NOW!

- In School: Math, statistics, and logic.
- After School: Ask if you can help a teacher plan a class field trip.
- Around Town: Observe how efficiently (or not!) mail is delivered in your neighborhood.

Next you meet with distribution managers and dispatchers, so that they can plan for additional transport for the increased delivery volume. Since you contract a trucking company and their business is a little slow, you are able to help the distribution manager negotiate a faster schedule for shipping a larger quantity of goods.

Finally you call your retailers' distribution centers to reserve warehouse space, and then you make sure space is reserved within the stores themselves. As product starts to pile up in the warehouse and then ship out, you monitor all points of the logistics plan you created until the last of the excess shipment has shipped. Time to adjust for the post-back-to-school supply sales lull.

Regardless of the endless potential responsibilities associated with this position, depending on an employer's needs, being a logistics planner in any company requires certain common characteristics. Since logistics planners work with many employees in a variety of areas of a company, it pays to have good people skills and be highly organized. A disorganized logistics planner will cost the company time and money, but will also directly affect others' abilities to do their jobs. Running a tight logistics ship lets you help everyone succeed.

Marketing Manager

Your company makes jeans. You, the marketing manager, have led many meetings about how to best promote a new men's jean. You study sales figures for your other men's jeans, and compare advertising to see what seemed to work. You have examined the new jean's projected production costs, and have chosen a price point that will be profitable and yet still affordable for customers. It is time to formulate a marketing plan to sell those jeans.

Marketing managers work hard to plan ahead. For a new product, planning may start with product development. As the product development manager decides what to produce, the marketing manager offers input about how particular new products might fare in the market. Once a new product idea is agreed upon, marketing managers must know everything about that product (production budgets, timelines, costs, and competing products) in order to attract customers and turn a worthwhile profit. Production managers can help establish budgets for making the product—the jeans, in this case—that guide marketing managers to make pricing and distribution decisions.

Marketing managers also help market researchers and advertising managers decide how to sell the product. You want to make

GET STARTED NOW!

- In School: Business classes, psychology, marketing, computer classes, communications, and speech.
- After School: Get involved in your school's marketing club or help start one. Find out about DECA, a student marketing association, at http://www.deca.org.
- Around Town: Go to a mall and compare different brands of the same type product. What makes some "cooler" than others?

a big splash with the new jean, so you meet with an ad agency to discuss different possibilities for launching it, and decide that a celebrity endorsement from an athlete might be a good idea, since the jeans are designed for an active lifestyle (they are tough and roomy!) and the general brand is already popular with buyers under 30.

The advertising agency's creative team helps brainstorm male celebrities who are likely to buy the jeans anyway, and you narrow down the possibilities. The ad agency would work with the celebrity and the agent until they reach a deal. During negotiations, you keep a close eye on the budget—an expensive celebrity endorsement means smaller profits.

After the jeans hit store shelves, the commercials air, the creative team posts viral ads featuring the celebrity, and a Facebook page pops up. Meanwhile, you gather important information by initiating more market research. You want to know how well the jeans are selling, whether they are selling online, which stores are having success, where sales are not meeting expectations, and what to do about it. Thanks to you and your team's efforts, your research and sales figures indicate that the launch is successful. The new jean is the best seller in your line.

Marketing managers stay on top of current trends. They must be aware of all aspects of creating and launching a product so that they can make decisions based on what they predict the market share will be. Looking into the future is hard work and requires long hours, and mistakes can be costly. With help from other departments, smart thinking, and a little luck, marketing managers can mean the difference between a product's failure and its success.

Market Researcher

You're on your favorite Web site when suddenly a banner ad catches your eye. It's for your favorite clothing store. You click on the ad, and it's offering you a 20 percent coupon if you answer a few questions. You take the survey, get the coupon, and a week later you're sporting the new jacket you've been eyeing.

This entire transaction was brought to you courtesy of market researchers. They studied the data and know that teens such as you frequently visit that Web site. They placed the ad because they want teens to come to the clothing store. Finally, they not only offered you an incentive to visit the store (the coupon), but they also got some valuable information from you, which they will use to further improve their products and advertising decisions. The end result? You got a great jacket for a good price and they got some great demographic data on their target market. What a deal!

Market researchers know a lot about consumers. They know we like our Cheerios boxes yellow and that we won't pay more than $10 for a paperback novel. They know our online shopping habits, whether we like Coke or Pepsi, and how many times a year we buy new shoes. Now you may think the job description for a market researcher calls for intense mind reading, but instead it requires

GET STARTED NOW!

- In School: Math, psychology, statistics, English, drama, public speaking.
- After School: Create a weekly column for the school newspaper based on student surveys you take. Be sure to include your analysis of the results of each poll.
- Around Town: Get involved in DECA (http://www. www.deca.org), a nonprofit organization that prepares emerging leaders and entrepreneurs for careers in marketing, finance, and more.

incredible research and analytical skills.

Most market researchers work for consulting firms, which are hired by all sorts of companies, from computer and car manufacturers to movie studios and politicians, to test consumers' reactions to their products and policies. The first part of the job is to make informed assumptions (e.g., Maybe Cheerios' boxes are yellow because it makes people feel alert in the morning), and then make sure you're asking the right questions. You'll collect the answers to the questions in many different ways, including surveys to either send out via mail or to use online, conducting telephone surveys, setting up focus groups of potential consumers, collecting data from Web sites and store scanners, doing taste tests at shopping malls, and more. Most survey and focus groups are divided by age group so as to better understand more specifically who is buying certain products and why.

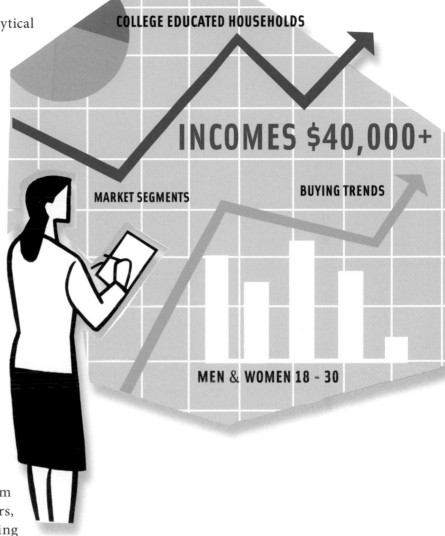

Once the questions have been asked and the answers tabulated, your job as market researcher really kicks into high gear. First you crunch the numbers. Then you analyze your statistics for trends. You'll also compare the product to the competitors'. Finally you write up your informed opinion as to how the company should change their product or advertising campaign to better meet customer demand. You may suggest lower retail prices, different packaging, more ads targeted to teens, or even drastic changes to the product. Your client wants to know why people buy or don't buy their products, and as their market researcher, you will not only be able to answer that question, but you'll tell them how to attract more and more customers.

Media Coordinator

You have read the latest articles about advertising trends and social media. You have conducted consumer surveys. These findings go into a report requested by your marketing manager, who has charged you with upgrading the media plan for your company's gaming system. Your company wants to make a big splash for the holiday season. The media blitz will begin in September as families decide which game system to buy for their lucky rug rats.

A media coordinator looks at the big picture and applies trend and consumer information to promoting each product or service. It is the media coordinator's job to decide how to best get the word out to increase sales. Media coordinators may spend within given budgets, or they may submit their own budgets based on the market and products' unique needs. In the gaming system example, social media is a relatively inexpensive way to reach typical gamers. You could launch a limited, online version of a game. You could invite gamers to post videos of themselves playing with friends. (Warning: Some games cause funny and extreme reactions during use!) Your costs would be limited to paying for Web site design and maintenance.

CAREER 411

Search It!
Media Communications Association–International at http://www.mca-i.org.

Surf It!
Find an example of a very successful media campaign at http://www.cavemanscrib.com/cavemanandme.

Read It!
Peruse an overview of media at http://www.admedia.org.

Learn It!
Minimum Education: Bachelor's degree.

Typical Majors: Communications, journalism, business, advertising, public relations.

Special Skills: Excellent computer and research skills, ability to work independently and as part of a team, superb communication skills, leadership abilities.

Earn It!
Median annual salary is $32,476.

(Source: http://www.salary.com)

GET STARTED NOW!

- In School: Communications, business classes, computer classes, public relations, journalism.
- After School: Prepare a media blitz for a school event or fund-raiser. Coordinate a team to make posters, create a Facebook events page, and post an ad on the school Web site.
- Around Town: Pay attention to how your town promotes local events like sports, theater, and the arts.

You may also pay for ads during tween and teen TV shows to reach kids who stay off the computer. To target a younger crowd, you could have a fast food company create plastic characters for kids' meal giveaways.

For a product like banking services, media coordinating may target different channels. Banking customers may not respond as readily to social media when deciding where to invest their money. Print ads in financial magazines or direct mail will help reinforce the message. TV ads aired during the nightly news or shows geared toward the typical investor's demographic would also reach the target audience.

Media coordinators must know current advertising trends, which is challenging in this rapidly evolving industry. In addition to research, media coordinators meet with media company reps who can share information about how best to use different available outlets. Media coordinators report constantly changing media outlets to executives so that there is less of a learning curve when it comes time to make specific recommendations. (You do not want to present pricing for an advergame, only to have an execu-

IF YOU WERE. . .

As a media coordinator, how would you promote an upcoming Hollywood film?

. . . MAKE IT REAL!

Go to Rotten Tomatoes (http://www.rottentomatoes.com) and scroll down to the "Coming Soon" section. Choose a movie that sounds interesting, and write a media plan for how to promote it. The type of movie you choose will be a big factor in how it's promoted. When you finish, search for promotions of this movie and see how your plan stacks up against what was actually done by the film studio's media team.

tive ask, "What is an advergame?") Media coordinators work with pub-lic relations managers to time events in relation to new advertising. And once media outlets are chosen, the media coordinator may liaise between the marketing department and various media companies.

Media coordinators depend on reliable and up-to-date infor-mation to do their jobs, and they must be adept at passing this information on. With the help of a skilled media coordinator, a company's products and services receive the customer attention they deserve.

Mediator

CAREER 411

Search It!
Association for Conflict Resolution at http:www.acrnet.org and American Arbitration Association at http://www.adr.org.

Surf It!
Go to http://highschoolmediator.com for a blog for teenagers, parents, and teachers concerned about high school issues and interested in solutions and best practices.

Read It!
See http://www.mediate.com for articles, news, and career advice for mediators.

Learn It!
Minimum Education: Bachelor's degree preferred, although not required.
Typical Majors: Public policy, law, government, child development, sociology.
Special Skills: Excellent communication skills, adept at negotiation and problem solving, impartial and diplomatic.

Earn It!
Median annual salary is $53,000.
(Source: U.S. Department of Labor)

Sometimes when two people are having a legal dispute, instead of running for the lawyers, they call in an impartial third party to help them resolve the conflict. Called a mediator, this person interviews both parties, finds out what they each want to get out of this process, and then, without thinking of labeling a winner and a loser, goes about helping the two sides reach a mutual agreement in which they both feel like winners. The mediator never takes sides, doesn't get personally involved in the dispute, and never forces a solution upon the disagreeing parties. These mediators sort through the differences between the two sides and find the common ground upon which they can help forge lasting solutions. Schools, families, divorcing couples, business partners, and others rely on mediators for an inexpensive, less acrimonious solution. Recently corporations have begun to hire mediators (both in-house and from outside firms) to help solve problems within their own organizations.

Mediators hired to work at companies may deal with labor, management, health care, morale, and other policy issues. And like the mediators working in other venues, mediators in businesses must also be neutral, impartial, and 100 percent engaged in helping the two parties reach a long-term agreement that satisfies all. Sometimes mediators are called in when companies merge and two sets

GET STARTED NOW!

- In School: English, communications, psychology, history.
- After School: Volunteer for your school's peer mediation organization. If your school doesn't have one, work on starting one.
- Around Town: Volunteer for any available community mediation programs.

of executives
need to learn
how to work
together. In that
instance, a mediator would come in and, instead of telling them
how to do their jobs, he would bring the two teams together and
guide them as they carve out their own solutions. Most companies
feel that by putting opposing sides of an issue in charge of the
solution, they have a vested interest in making sure that solution
works long after the mediator has moved on.

Mediators might also be hired to help foster positive communication between employees within a department or between two
or more departments that rely on each other to get their jobs done.
Other scenarios may include disputes between managers and
employees, arguments between labor unions and companies, and
complex issues between two companies that are merging. And
in each case, a good mediator won't just help to solve the direct
problem, but will seek to give the disagreeing parties the tools they
need to handle difficulties that arise in the future. As a mediator,
you'll rely on your creative problem-solving skills to get people
who don't necessarily want to cooperate and compromise to not

only do both, but also to end up feeling pretty good about getting to the root of the problems.

Each state has a different requirement for becoming a mediator, so while you don't need a law degree to mediate, it does pay to be knowledgeable about legal issues, and you may have to take courses to become certified or licensed. In fact, businesses looking to hire mediators will often only hire someone with experience as well as state certification or licensure.

Meeting and Convention Planner

Conventions and meetings happen for all kinds of reasons: from fan club gatherings, to world leaders meeting about global issues, to corporate executives planning a company's future. Some meetings are for small groups, while thousands may attend conventions. Whether working for the group planning the convention or for a venue that books conventions and meetings, a meeting and convention planner strives to make every gathering successful.

The fact that no two meetings or conventions are exactly alike keeps planners on their toes. For example, consider a fansite dedicated to a (very) famous book series that has spawned rock bands, podcasts, movies, and toys. That fansite hires a convention planner to oversee their second convention. The planner meets with fansite executives and fans, and learns that the attendees want to participate in discussion panels and workshops, and mingle in costume at a rock concert. (The underlying purpose of the convention is to sustain the fansite's visitor momentum so advertisers will continue to pay for space.) The planner gets an attendance estimate, and then organizes assistants to carry out various tasks.

Next the planner evaluates potential venues for location, suitability, capacity, availability, nearby hotels, prices, and perks

GET STARTED NOW!

- In School: Hospitality classes, business and marketing, communications.
- After School: Organize a special event at your school, like multicultural night or science night. Or volunteer to help plan the school science fair.
- Around Town: Volunteer at your local book or art festival.

CAREER 411

Search It!
Convention Industry Council at http://www.conventionindustry.org or Meeting Professionals International at http://www.mpiweb.org.

Surf It!
Use an Internet browser to find the meetings and convention bureau in your town or a nearby big city.

Read It!
Find all kinds of resources at the Meetings and Conventions Web site: http://www.meetings-conventions.com.

Learn It!
Minimum Education: Bachelor's degree.

Typical Majors: Hospitality-related careers, communications, business, management.

Special Skills: Ability to work with a variety of people, excellent communication and organizational skills, attentive to detail, multitasker, deadline oriented, budgeting abilities, strong critical thinking skills.

Earn It!
Median annual salary is $44,780.
(Source: U.S. Department of Labor)

offered. For example, a hotel without a ballroom cannot house a rock concert. A convention center in a town with no airport will be hard to reach. The planner weeds out these possibilities and presents a short list of suitable venues to fansite executives. When the site is chosen, the planner meets with venue staff about the logistics: transportation, traffic flow, locations for workshops and the concert, signage, programs, audiovisual equipment rental, etc. If the meeting is in a hotel, the venue will reserve a block of rooms; if not, they will suggest nearby hotels. The planner may obtain labor agreements, fire department permits to govern exhibits and capacity, and health department permits for food vendors.

A meeting and convention planner may help recruit workshop leaders. (That means recruiting bands for the concert, too.) The planner also oversees negotiating and signing service contracts, security, printing badges and event passes, recruiting volunteers, finding sponsors, and marketing. The planner might have a Web designer create an online signup and payment system.

During the convention, the planner troubleshoots problems: room shortages, a late lecturer, a fire alarm, etc. Afterward, most planners use surveys to gather feedback for future conventions. The planner finalizes payments for all goods and services, and will plan a post-convention meeting with fansite executives to review results—and celebrate!

For many planners, travel is a regular task, unless the planner specializes in organizing virtual meetings. The work hours are very long just before, during, and after a convention. Keeping up with so many details while keeping corporations and attendees happy can be grueling, but a successful event is a terrific reward.

Office Manager

At some companies, employees get bogged down with extraneous tasks. They sort all of the mail. They run out of supplies and have to order new ones. They answer all phone calls and type and send out letters. They pack, ship, and track packages. When the workload gets too large to handle, they scout out and train temps. It is difficult for them to find time to do the jobs they were hired to do. This is not the case at your company. You are an office manager, and you run a tight ship, so that others in your office are free to do their jobs. They do not know what they would do without you.

Office managers provide important support services. Depending on the company, their duties vary widely, but certain key functions are part of most office managers' jobs. One main function is filing paperwork. In most companies, paper orders, correspondence, shipping and receiving records, job applications, worker's compensation requests, employee review forms, office supply orders, and any other papers that record expenses or go into an employee's permanent record must be filed appropriately. A good office manager devises the filing system and helps others maintain it.

Another important responsibility is regulating support staff's secretarial functions, such as maintaining executive calendars and

GET STARTED NOW!

- In School: Word processing and other computer classes, English, accounting, business.
- After School: Volunteer in your school office or run for class secretary.
- Around Town: Find new ways to keep your life organized at home and at school.

IF YOU WERE. . .

As an office manager, how would you market yourself for your next job interview?

. . . MAKE IT REAL!

Visit Resume resource (http://www.resume-resource. com/exman7.html) to look at the sample office manager résumé. Create a résumé using your own relevant skills and experience in place of those on the template. The résumé should show that you are responsible, organized, and efficient. If you lack experience, volunteer or find a job that will help you acquire more skills.

setting appointments; routing mail and phone calls; and keeping up with mail, e-mail, and faxes, including billing and payments. When the support staff's workload is too great, the office manager often hires and trains new staff to do the extra work. If there are any disputes between support staff or complaints about job performance, the office manager handles these, too.

Office managers can also order office supplies, from staples and paperclips to furniture and larger equipment. If a printer breaks, or the office cubicles are falling apart, or the sticky notes run out, the office manager may be in charge of selecting and ordering new equipment.

Finally office managers update senior management on everything from staff performance reviews to financial reports. They pass along requests for staffing, supplies, and equipment. They also take minutes in meetings, and then distribute minutes to participants afterward. Most office managers participate in organizational policy and procedural meetings, since it is the office manager who will train staff members to follow these procedures.

Many companies feel that good office managers are worth their weight in gold. If senior managers are very demanding, or if there is a lot of turnover or employee conflict, this job can be stressful. If a company has to make budget cuts, office workers are often the first to go, and executives have to start handling their own details. But a highly organized, efficient, and firm but personable office manager can earn respect and job security, and can often advance in a company.

Payroll Manager

This Friday is payday and you are scrambling to enter timesheets. Of course you spent half of your morning tracking down managers whose employees have not yet entered their time, and you spent the other half of your morning terminating three employees' payroll entries because they resigned. You spent another half adding six new employees and keying in three employee transfers to other departments. Wait, that's one-and-a-half mornings. No wonder you are behind!

Whether they work internally at a company or are outsourced from a company that does nothing but maintain corporate payrolls, payroll managers ensure that employees get paid. In order to do this, they set up employee files in the payroll system and track and compile timesheets. Some companies have a computerized time-tracking system, while other companies still use paper and pencil to keep track of employees' time. Some companies rely on time clocks and time cards. Employees punch time cards each day as they arrive, break for lunch, and leave. Regardless of the system used, a payroll manager must verify time worked, vacation time and absences, overtime, and wages. Since this is a lot of information to keep track of for each employee and it changes every week,

GET STARTED NOW!

- In School: Math, business, accounting, and statistics.
- After School: Run for class treasurer or volunteer to manage the finances of a favorite after-school club.
- Around Town: Pay attention to the different kinds of services that banks in your town offer to business clients.

payroll managers often look to department managers to turn over verified time information.

Payroll managers keep track of difficult, confusing information, such as W4 tax forms for all employees, accrued vacation and sick days, withholdings (and matching contributions) for social security and Medicare, insurance, workers' compensation contributions, state and federal income tax, tax exemptions, wage garnishments (usually to recover debt or child support), health insurance, monies diverted into IRA or other savings accounts, union dues, and other adjustments that are made to gross pay.

Once the payroll manager verifies all of the information above, it is time to record it. Payroll managers must have excellent data entry skills, since something as simple as an extra zero can make a big difference in a paycheck—oops! The payroll manager enters employee time into a ledger or into the

TAXES

578.44
52.67
356.66
833.24
45.33

TIME CARD
090914 / 092014

Sept 9	
Sept 10	10.25
Sept 11	9.50
Sept 12	8.75
Sept 13	11.00
	10.25
Sept 16	
Sept 17	7.50

WAGES

134,558.00
34,356.00
5,778.00
456.98
23,890.77
5,678.00
35,667.99

EARNINGS

1003554

CORP INC.
13200 CORPORATE AVE.
MAYVILLE, NY 20022

$2110.88

PAY TO: DAVID JOHNSON

AMOUNT: TWO THOUSAND ONE HUNDRED TEN   88 /100 DOLLARS

NOTE

09 453678 00989 16678

12.50
8.25
9.50
11.50
12.25

54.00

IF YOU WERE. . .

As a payroll manager, how could you set a good example by keeping a neat and accurate time sheet?

. . . MAKE IT REAL!

Keep a time sheet of your schoolwork for a week. Open and print a blank Excel or other spreadsheet document, or track your time on the computer. Label columns with these headings: date, task, subject, start time, and end time. For one week, keep track of the time you spend in each class, on homework, and other activities. Use this data to your advantage. Which class takes the most time? Which class takes the least?

computer—usually via a payroll software program—and reviews everything for accuracy. Upon approval, the company's bank can release payment, either through paper paychecks or automated electronic deposits.

Payroll managers make it possible for people to make a living at their jobs, obtain health insurance, and save for retirement. Their attention to detail and thoroughness help ensure that people's wages are correctly distributed at the appropriate time. And hey, they get to pay themselves, too!

Project Manager

CAREER 411

Search It!
The International Community for Project Managers at http://www.theicpm.com.

Surf It!
Check out some project management tools at http://www.businessballs.com.

Read It!
Brush up on project management skills at http://www.pmi.org/Knowledge-Center.aspx.

Learn It!
Minimum Education:
Bachelor's degree.

Typical Majors: Business, accounting and finance, marketing and advertising, communications. Also, majors in a specific area where project management is an option, like IT or construction, are helpful.

Special Skills: Ability to multitask, ability to work well with all kinds of people, strong leadership and organizational skills, stress management skills, attentive to detail.

Earn It!
Median annual salary is $82,330 (for a construction project manager; pay varies by field). (Source: U.S. Department of Labor)

Project managers' duties vary with the assignment and the company, but the basics are the same. At the beginning of a project, the project manager must assess the project's goals. It helps to have a kickoff meeting to clarify the project's purpose, as well as what results supervisors expect. In that meeting the project manager gathers information about budgets, deadlines, project team members and their duties, and reporting and authority.

A next logical step would be to meet with others on the project team to assign tasks and deadlines, and convey the overall vision and goals for the project. Team members may be subordinates or superiors, and may work in different departments, but they all report to the project manager. The project manager follows progress, tracks spending, enforces deadlines, and informs superiors of progress and any difficulties that arise.

As a project manager for a construction company, you might be a general contractor who works for a large construction corporation. Your project? Oversee the construction of a new school. You would first meet with the architect, your supervisor, the principal, and representatives from the school system to review the plans and visit the job site. You would discuss budgets, a start date, and a deadline. Next you and your supervisor would plan to schedule subcontractors from your company, or from outside

GET STARTED NOW!

- In School: Business, marketing, communication, and computer classes.
- After School: Volunteer to head up a school fund-raiser or run for student council.
- Around Town: Get involved with a local charity or nonprofit organization.

sources. Your team members would be those subcontractors: a demolition crew (to tear down the old school), graders, builders, roofers, electricians, plumbers, playground installers, landscapers, etc. As the project manager, you schedule their work in the right order and for the right amount of time, so that you do not have the electrician and the plumber stumbling over each other, or landscapers waiting around for graders. As the project manager and general contractor, you are ultimately responsible for the quality of the subcontractors' work, and for meeting deadlines and staying on budget. If you do your job of ensuring that the subcontractors do their jobs on time and correctly, the kids will enjoy a new school by the beginning of the following school year, and not in the middle of it.

For a project manager, every new project is a new beginning. In some corporations, project management creates opportunities to learn and to make new contacts, which can make you an ideal candidate for advancement. Even though starting a new project can be daunting, completing a project successfully is a great reason to celebrate.

Public Relations Manager

You pass the chimps, wave to the elephants, and watch snacking giraffes. It's just another day on your way to the office as the zoo's public relations (PR) manager. It is your job to disseminate information that improves community relations and casts the zoo in the best possible light. You have plenty of good zoo news to share.

Whether PR managers work for PR firms or in-house for a corporation, it is their job to ensure that a corporation's public image is well represented. They oversee external communication to the media, the government, and the public. They often write press releases or speak to the press about company news, and may create media kits (folders of company information) for potential investors or business partners. PR managers oversee in-house writers and collaborate with social media managers and Web site designers to ensure that the company releases consistent, truthful information. PR managers may also write speeches for top executives, or even coach employees about dealing with the public. If the media or a government agency has questions about expenditures, corporate practices, or employee activities, the PR manager may find the answers, and will almost certainly be the one to respond.

GET STARTED NOW!

- In School: Public relations, journalism, business and marketing, communications, psychology, computer classes.
- After School: Help publicize a school event, such as a pep rally or big game, or a school fund-raiser.
- Around Town: Volunteer to work with the PR committee at a nonprofit that is sponsoring a neighborhood open house, festival, or other event.

CAREER 411

Search It!
Public Relations Student Society of America at http://www.prssa.org.

Surf It!
Visit a real zoo public relation's Web page at http://media.sandiegozoo.org.

Read It!
Check out the latest media releases at PR Newswire (http://www.prnewswire.com).

Learn It!
Minimum Education: Bachelor's degree.

Typical Majors: Public relations, journalism, business, communications.

Special Skills: Creativity, excellent communication skills, ability to handle stress, computer skills, writing proficiency, leadership skills.

Earn It!
Median annual salary is $89,690.

(Source: U.S. Department of Labor)

Finally, a PR manager approves communication budgets.

When corporations stumble by making bad decisions or having bad luck, the PR manager has the difficult job of releasing information to a hostile public and the media. As the zoo's PR manager, you may troubleshoot sticky situations, for example, if one of the polar bears dies. The public will be understandably upset at the loss of a favorite—and endangered—animal. It is always best for the PR manager to be the one to break sad news, so you quickly learn that the polar bear was elderly and had kidney failure, and that zookeepers did all that they could to save him before euthanizing him to end his suffering. You get a brief statement from the zoo president, and then you feed the information through several channels. You also have the Web designer post a memorial video and condolences wall.

When things run smoothly, PR is enjoyable and can be very creative. As the zoo's PR manager, you may sponsor online animal drawing contests (Win free passes!), or write a press release about the zoo's new night hours. You post special "interviews" with newly acquired animals. You schedule a corporate sponsor gala to thank supporters. When a nonprofit camp for children with special needs approaches you, you happily host them as the zoo's special guests. You share all good news with the shareholders and the public—it pays to advertise!

Good PR managers employ honesty and good judgment as they keep an eye on everything to make sure that things go smoothly. When that does not happen, the PR manager advises everyone and helps the company weather the storm.

Purchasing Agent

Your company has finalized designs for the spring furniture market. It is time for you, the manufacturer's purchasing agent, to spring into action and acquire raw materials for the furniture factories. You create a bill of materials (BOM) for the wood, copper and iron, granite, glass, and textiles that make up each chair, couch, and other pieces in the new line. You also handle purchasing finished goods: computers and furniture, office supplies, finishing equipment, and shipping vehicles. You strive to find the best deals on anything your company needs.

The purchasing agent first learns what raw materials (stone, glass, wood, etc.) are needed for production, then current market values for each item, and uses this information to narrow down potential suppliers. In addition to looking for a high-quality selection, the agent evaluates suppliers' reliability and their reputation with other customers, compares pricing, and interviews suppliers about extra services they might provide.

After choosing suppliers, the agent negotiates contracts that outline all agreements between each selected supplier and the purchasing agent's employer. Contracts usually include quan-

GET STARTED NOW!

- In School: Marketing, business, economics, math, and computer classes.
- After School: Think about a big-ticket item you want to buy, like a new video game system or a car. Do some research online to find the best price for your item.
- Around Town: Visit a local store that has a stockroom, and ask for a tour. Talk with the store manager about how she controls the flow of goods in the stockroom.

tities of goods and materials to be purchased, delivery dates, acceptable conditions for those goods or materials, and final pricing. Both parties sign the contract, and the supplier prepares and ships the materials and goods according to an agreed-upon schedule. Note that any corporation with a warehouse relies on a purchasing agent to plan carefully and ensure that deliveries arrive on a schedule to keep warehouses stocked with finished goods.

An empty warehouse means too few goods have been produced, and customers will get grouchy about late orders. A crowded warehouse means too many goods are lying around—they may be wasted if there are too few orders. A purchasing agent must strike the right balance between too much and too little when scheduling shipments. (Agents who purchase goods for resale must contend with warehouse storage, too. Warehousing costs money, so timing matters when shipping goods in and out of a warehouse.)

A purchasing agent's work does not end with the signed contract. The agent follows up with end users of goods and materials. Did they arrive on time? Were they in acceptable condition? For example, if the furniture company's glass tabletops arrive chipped and scratched, it is the purchasing agent's job to return them to the supplier and negotiate a new shipment. Since late or damaged shipments usually mean that a company gets a refund or other compensation, the purchasing agent must keep a thorough record of the condition and timing of shipments.

Purchasing requires a lot of task juggling and organization. Making contacts among suppliers is an important part of the job. Negotiation skills are important, since purchasing managers build long-term relationships as they make deals. Be prepared to "shake on it"—but get a signed contract too.

Risk Manager

Running a corporation means taking risks. There is just no getting around it. Investments fail. Accidents happen. Mother Nature wreaks havoc. A risk manager actively prepares for and prevents loss. In hiring a good risk manager, a company knows it has done all it can to protect itself.

There are many kinds of loss. Investment loss happens when a company's investments fail. For example, imagine that a bank has purchased home mortgages, but thousands of people lose their jobs, default on their mortgages, and abandon their houses. The bank is stuck with a lot of houses that will not sell, and no incoming mortgage payments. Without the mortgage payment money, the bank struggles with cash flow.

Another type of loss happens when employees go on strike. Say a taxi company's drivers belong to a union. If the company and the union cannot agree about a pay raise for the cab drivers, the union may strike, halting taxi service until the company gives in to some demands. No taxis means lost revenue, and the company will struggle with expenses as it loses customers, too.

Other loss results from accidents or catastrophes. The oil spill in the Gulf of Mexico in 2010 is a perfect example. After the oil rig explosion, British Petroleum (BP) faced massive losses due to

CAREER 411

 Search It!
Risk and Insurance Management Society at http://www.rims.org.

 Surf It!
Play Stop Disasters! (http://www.stopdisastersgame.org/en/home.html) and try your hand at averting the worst from volcanoes, fires, floods, and storms.

 Read It!
Find out how companies and individuals minimize health care risk at http://health.howstuffworks.com/medicine/healthcare/insurance/health-insurance.htm.

 Learn It!
Minimum Education: Bachelor's degree plus specialized training.
Typical Majors: Finance, business, insurance, real estate, or pre-law.
Special Skills: Excellent analytical and organizational skills, ability to work well under pressure and handle stress, superb communication skills, time management skills, ability to meet deadlines, planning skills.

 Earn It!
Median annual salary is $58,350.
(Source: U.S. Department of Labor)

GET STARTED NOW!

- In School: Math, business, statistics, logic.
- After School: Practice risk management at home by creating a disaster plan for your family in case of fire.
- Around Town: Ask permission to open a savings account. Save money each month in case of emergency.

CYBER ATTACK

PRODUCT LIABILITY

INDUSTRIAL ESPIONAGE

OPERATIONS INTERRUPTION

EMPLOYEE LAWSUITS

cleanup costs, payment to Gulf residents, and from customers who boycotted BP gas stations.

Most risk managers advise companies on how to purchase insurance to offset loss, but a risk manager's job is to do everything possible to prevent loss in the first place. As a risk manager for the bank, you notice that many of the purchased mortgages have adjustable rates, which means that more people will default as interest rates are rising. You might advise executives to create a mortgage counseling program for new homeowners, and encourage current homeowners to refinance to fixed-rate mortgages. For the taxi company, you would make sure there was plenty of insurance to cover lost revenue during a strike, and as a result of regular meetings with union bosses, you would advise executives to be proactive about cab driver wage negotiations.

For a company like BP, part of your job as a risk manager would be to minimize risks associated with handling gasoline and other hazardous materials. You would work with rig safety inspectors and regulators to ensure that employees follow safety procedures. You would also work with insurers, PR managers, and investors to minimize financial damage in the face of a disaster.

Risk managers must use expert advice, data and statistical analysis, common sense, and even intuition to assess many kinds of risk. In risk management, it pays to anticipate problems, but just as important is an ability to communicate those risks with the right amount of urgency. While they cannot always prevent problems, good risk managers are as prepared as possible for whatever happens next.

EXPERIMENT WITH SUCCESS

Stop! Hold it right there. You are so not ready to experiment with success until you have explored your way to a career idea that makes you wonder, "Is this one right for me?"

You will know you are ready to take things to the next level when you are still curious about a specific career idea even after you have used the tools featured in Section Two to:

- Investigate that career idea so thoroughly that you know almost as much about what it's like as someone who is already doing it
- Complete a Hire Yourself activity with impressive results

If, after all that, you still want to know more, this section is where you can crank things up by:

- Talking with people who already have careers like the one you want
- Looking at different types of employment situations where people get paid to do what you want to do
- Figuring out a few next steps for getting from where you are now (high school) to where you want to go (a successful career)

In other words, you are going to:

- ASK for advice and start building a career-boosting network
- ASSESS a variety of future workplace options
- ADDRESS options to make the most of now to get ready for a successful future

ASK for Advice and Start Building a Career–Boosting Network

There's nothing like going straight to the source to find out what a specific career is really like. After all, who's more likely to have the inside scoop on the real deal than someone who has actually "been there, done that." It is surprisingly easy to get most people talking about their careers. All you have to do is ask.

E-mail, Twitter, Facebook, and other cool social networking tools now make it easier than ever to touch base with almost any expert in the world for advice and information. But whether you conduct your career chats the old-fashioned way with face-to-face conversations or via the latest and greatest technologies, the following tips will help you make a good first impression.

1 **Practice with people you already know.** Start asking parents, relatives, neighbors, and other trusted adults to talk about what their work is really like, and you're likely to be amazed by what you find out.

2 Think about what you want to know before you start asking questions. Jot down a few questions that you can refer to if you get nervous or the conversation starts to lag. Keep the conversation flowing by asking open-ended questions that require more than simple yes or no answers like:

- Tell me about...
- How do you feel about...?
- What was it like...?

3 Be polite, professional, and considerate of the person's time. In other words, don't be a pest! Just because you can access any person, any place, any time doesn't mean that you should.

4 Seek answers *and* advice. Make the most of any opportunity to learn from other people's successes and mistakes. Be sure to ask them what they know now that they wish they had known when they were your age.

You may want to add some of these questions to your interviews:

- How do your childhood interests relate to your choice of career path?
- How did you first learn about the job you have today?
- In what ways is your job different from how you expected it to be?
- What is a typical day on the job like for you?
- What are the best and worst parts of your job?

- If anything were possible, how would you change your job description?
- What kinds of people do you usually meet in your work?
- How is your product made (or service delivered)?
- What other kinds of professionals work here?
- Tell me about the changes you have seen in your industry over the years. What do you see as the future of the industry?

5 Keep your career-information network growing.
Conclude each interview with a sincere thank you and a request for recommendations about other people or resources to turn to for additional information.

CAREER CHATS

Think about who knows what you want to know. Use online news and professional association Web sites to identify experts in your field of interest. For extra help finding contact information, use Google to identify the person's company Web site or other professional affiliations. And, of course, do make use of the time-honored "friend of a friend of a friend" network to find contacts known to friends, parents, neighbors, teachers, and others who share an interest in helping you succeed.

Depending on each person's availability, interviews can be arranged onsite at a person's place of employment (with parental permission and supervision only), via a prescheduled phone conversation, or online with e-mail, Skype, or other social networking tools. Find out which method is most convenient for the person you'd like to interview.

One note of encouragement (and caution) before you get started. Most people are more than happy to talk about their careers. After all, who doesn't like talking about themselves? So, on the one hand, you don't have to worry about asking since most people will say yes if they have the time. On the other hand, you'll want to be careful about who you contact. Take every precaution to make sure that every person is legit (as opposed to being certified creepers) and make sure that a trusted adult (such as a parent or teacher) has your back as you venture out into the real world.

With that said, use the following chart (or, if this book does not belong to you, create one like it) to keep track of whom you contact and what they say. Once you get the hang of it, use the same process to contact others who are likely to know what you need to know about your future career.

Contact Information

Name: _____

Company: _____

Title: _____

Company Web Site: _____

Preferred Contact Method: _____

❑ Phone _____

❑ E-mail _____

❑ Twitter _____

❑ Facebook _____

❑ Blog _____

❑ Other _____

CONTACT LOG		
Date/Time	Question	Answer

Lessons Learned

Nice as it is to talk to other people about their success, there's a point where you can't help but wonder what it all means for you. Here's your chance to apply what you've learned from your career chats to your own situation. Take a few minutes to think through your best answers to the following questions:

- What do you know about this career that you didn't know before?
- What kind of knowledge and skills do you need to acquire to prepare for a career like this?
- Are you more or less inclined to pursue this type of career? Why or why not?

ASSESS a Variety of Workplace Options

Employers come in all shapes and sizes. They run the gamut from huge multinational conglomerates to small mom-and-pop shops with a lot of options in-between. Big or small, before any employer agrees to hire you, they are going to want to know pretty much everything there is to know about you. Where did you go to school? What kind of grades did you make? What are your professional goals? Questions like these will keep flying until an employer is absolutely certain that you are the right choice for their company.

But guess what? It takes two to create a mutually beneficial employment relationship—an employer who gets what he needs and an employee who gets what he wants. In other words, that get-acquainted curiosity cuts both ways. It's just as important for you to find out if the company is a good fit for you as it is for them. After all, your success is their success and vice versa.

In most cases it's a bit early to decide on your ultimate employer with any precision. However, it's the perfect time to take a look at the options. Can you see yourself in the fast-paced world of a high-powered Fortune 500 firm? Are you better suited for an energetic, entrepreneurial, start-up company? Would you just as soon shuck the corporate world for a job that lets you work outdoors or, perhaps, one that requires a lot of travel?

Figuring out what kind of environment you want to work in is almost as important as figuring out what you want to do. Fortunately the Internet makes scouting out workplace options just a few mouse clicks away. Use the following tips to find out more about employers who hire people to do the kind of work you want to do.

- **Surf the Web** to seek out companies according to industry, career type, or geographic location. For instance, a quick Google search for "agribusiness" is likely to yield a list of resources that includes the U.S. Department of Agriculture

to companies specializing in everything from beverages and beehives to snack foods and seeds.

- **Find a List** that meets some sort of criteria. Want to work for one of the nation's biggest, most successful companies? Run a search for Fortune 500 companies at http://www.forbes.com. Want to find an exciting, up-and-coming company? Look for a list of "fastest growing companies" at http://www.inc.com or http://money.cnn.com. Want to find a company that treats its employees especially well? Track down a list of great places to work at http://www.greatplacestowork.com. Prefer a family-friendly company? Check out Working Mother's lists of bests at http://www.workingmother.com/best-companies.

- **Visit Company Web Sites** to compare opportunities associated with different kinds of employment situations—government, corporate, and small business, for instance. Simply run a search for the name of any company you want to know about— even most small companies have a Web site these days. Be sure to check out the current "careers" or "job listings" sections to get a sense of what the company looks for and offers prospective employees. Also use the Google news feature to look for current newsworthy articles about a prospective employer.

How a company presents itself online offers an interesting perspective of what the company's culture might be like. These types of online resources also offer a great way to find out more about a company's products and services, mission, values, clients, and reputation. The bonus is all the contact names and details you can use to seek out additional information.

Employer Profiles

Ready for a little cyber-snooping? Go online to track down information about three different types of employers: **a major corporation** (think Fortune 500); **a small business** (think entrepreneurial); and **a government agency** (think local, state, or federal) that offers opportunities associated with the career pathway you'd like to pursue. Use the following chart to record your discoveries and compare the results.

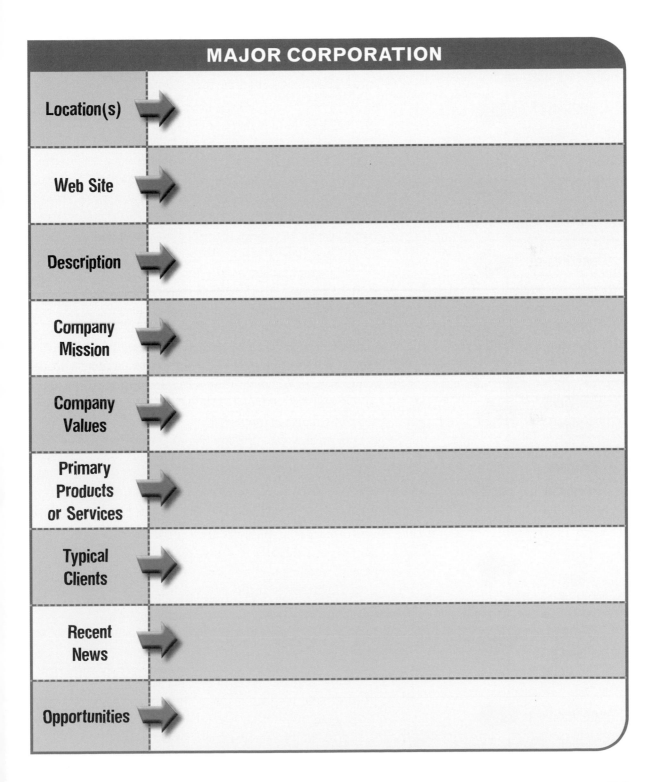

MAJOR CORPORATION

Location(s)	
Web Site	
Description	
Company Mission	
Company Values	
Primary Products or Services	
Typical Clients	
Recent News	
Opportunities	

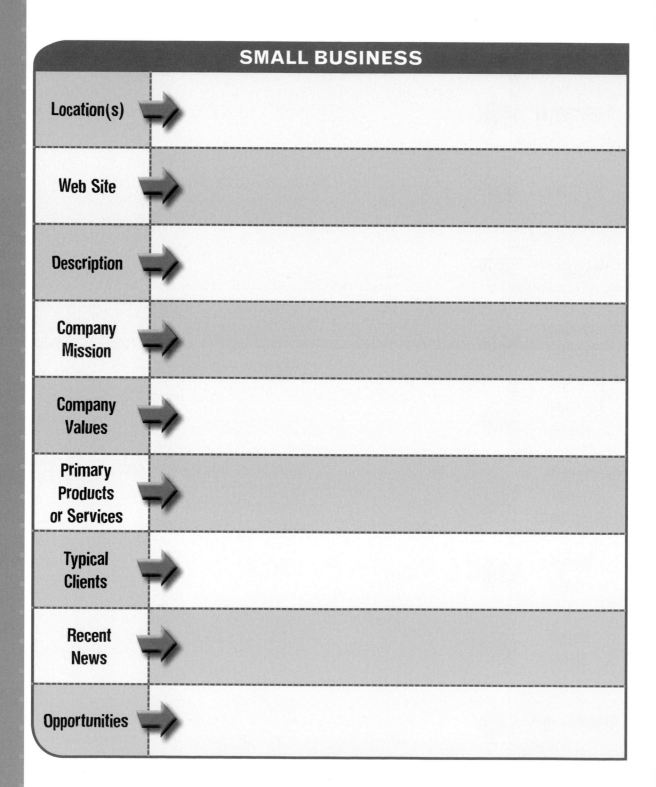

SMALL BUSINESS

Location(s)	
Web Site	
Description	
Company Mission	
Company Values	
Primary Products or Services	
Typical Clients	
Recent News	
Opportunities	

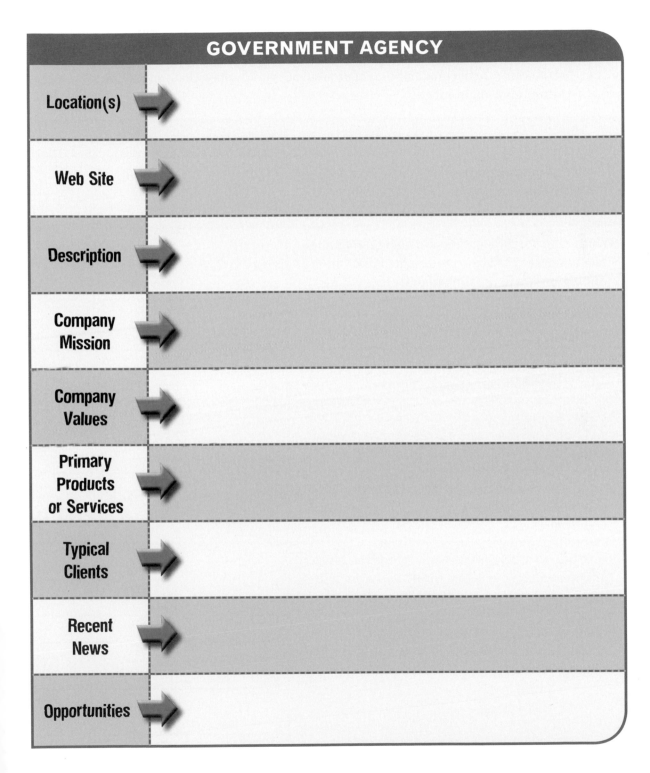

GOVERNMENT AGENCY

Location(s)	
Web Site	
Description	
Company Mission	
Company Values	
Primary Products or Services	
Typical Clients	
Recent News	
Opportunities	

Lessons Learned

Take time out to think through what you've learned about your workplace preferences. Use the following chart to compare the pros and cons of each situation and apply what you learned to what you want in a future work environment.

	Major Corporation
Based on your first impression of the company's Web site, how would you describe each employer?	
What factor(s) did you find most appealing about each company? (Size, geographic location, opportunities for advancement, etc.)	
What factor(s) did you like least about the company?	
What (if any) types of employment opportunities interested you most at each company?	
In what ways does (or doesn't) the company's mission statement and values align with what matters most to you in a future career?	
Would you be comfortable devoting your time and talents to help this company succeed? Why or why not?	
If you had to choose between these three types of employers, which type would you expect to enjoy working for the most? Why?	
Based on what you've learned through this process, what three factors have you identified as essential attributes of a future employer?	1 _____ 2 _____ 3 _____

Small Business	Government Agency
1 _____	1 _____
2 _____	2 _____
3 _____	3 _____

ADDRESS Options to Make the Most of Now

Well—big sigh of relief—you've almost made it through the entire Discover, Explore, Experiment process. This time and effort represent a huge investment in your future and has introduced a process you can rely on to guide you through a lifetime of career decisions.

But, you may well be wondering: "How do I get from here to there?"

Good question.

The answer? One step at a time.

No matter if you are moving full steam ahead toward a particular career or still meandering through the options—even if you are freaking out with indecision—here's what to do next: Map out a plan!

Your plan does not have to be set in stone with no wiggle room to take advantage of new opportunities. Instead it should move you forward along the pathway you choose to pursue and provide solid tools that prepare you to make the most of every opportunity that comes your way.

The first approach is complicated and, face it, a bit unrealistic. After all, who knows how your interests and talents will evolve over time? It's impossible to predict what kinds of as-yet-unheard-of opportunities will emerge in the future. Think about it. Did your great-grandparents dream of becoming computer programmers or Webmasters? Probably not. Chances are personal computers were an unimaginable innovation when they were making career choices. Long story short, the perfect career for you may not even exist yet.

The second approach is simple and leaves plenty of room for change as life and experience present new opportunities. It's not an attempt to plot out every last detail of your entire life. Instead, focus on making the most of now. What can you do now to get ready for a successful future? How can you get out of "stuck mode" and inch just a little closer to some actual choices?

The first thing you can do is to make the most of the opportunities waiting right under your nose for you to find them. These opportunities include wonderful new high school options designed to help students like you connect academic learning to real-world opportunities. Career academies, career pathways, career and technical education opportunities, and early college programs are just a few ways you can make the most of now.

Joining after-school clubs, volunteering for a cause you care about, and even getting a part-time job are other ways you can expand your horizons and gain useful experience. If it's information you are after, why not try some job shadowing or an internship at a local company of interest? Of course it goes without saying that getting good grades and staying out of trouble are helpful strategies, too.

There is so much you can do today to prepare for a brighter future. So why are you still sitting there? Start researching the options so you can map out a few next steps to get you where you want to go.

Next Stop Options

X marks the spot. You are here in high school. How do you get from high school to a successful career? Find out all you can about various options offered at your school or in your community. Use the following checklist of options to keep track of details about each opportunity. You'll get a chance to map out specific next steps later.

OPTIONS

What kinds of career academies, career pathways, career and technical education, early college, or other special academic and career readiness programs does your school offer that fit with your career aspirations?

Ask your school adviser or guidance counselor to help you sort out which options are right for you.

What kinds of core academic courses can you take to prepare for a specific career pathway?

For instance, advanced math and science courses are good choices for someone looking toward a career in engineering.

What kinds of electives can you fit into your schedule to explore different kinds of opportunities?

For instance, environmental studies is a good choice for someone considering a green career.

What clubs and after-school activities provide opportunities to explore various career interests?

For instance, 4-H for someone interested in agriculture or natural resources; science competitions for future scientists; Future Business Leaders of America for business wannabes.

What local businesses offer opportunities for firsthand observations of how people do what you want to do?

Ask your school adviser or guidance counselor about job shadowing opportunities. Or go online to http://www.jobshadow.com to find out about local job shadowing opportunities.

What kinds of internship opportunities are available for students to get real-world work experiences?

Talk to your school adviser or guidance counselor about internship opportunities at your school.

Where can you volunteer to help further a favorite cause while, at the same time, building useful skills and experience?

Talk with the leader of a favorite community or religious organization about volunteer opportunities or go online to explore service learning options at http://www.learnandserve.gov.

What does your high school do to introduce students to various college, military, and other career training programs?

Ask your school adviser or guidance counselor for a schedule of college visits, career fairs, and other resources.

YOUR CHOICES
Academic and Career Readiness Programs
Core Academic Courses
Elective Courses
Clubs and After-School Activities
Job Shadowing Opportunities
Internships
Volunteer Experiences
College and Career Training Programs

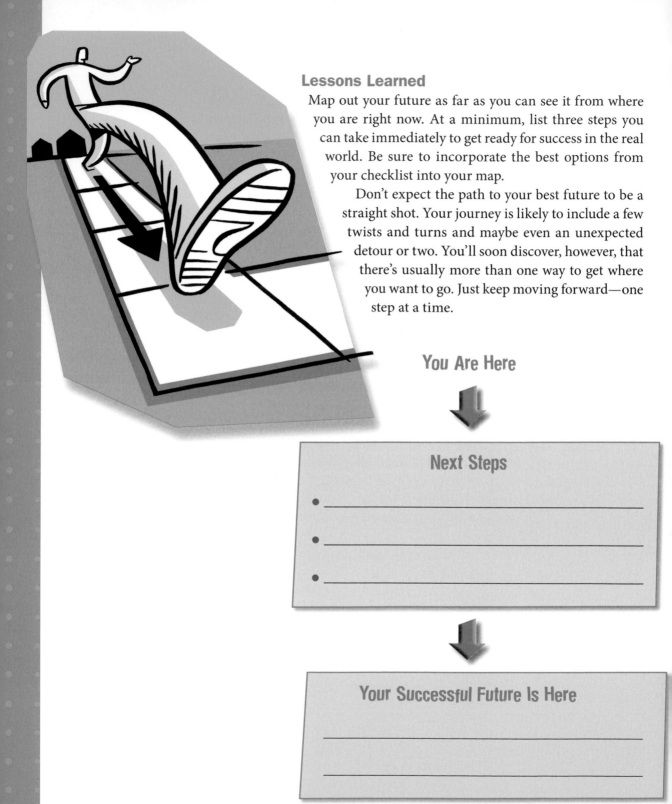

Lessons Learned

Map out your future as far as you can see it from where you are right now. At a minimum, list three steps you can take immediately to get ready for success in the real world. Be sure to incorporate the best options from your checklist into your map.

Don't expect the path to your best future to be a straight shot. Your journey is likely to include a few twists and turns and maybe even an unexpected detour or two. You'll soon discover, however, that there's usually more than one way to get where you want to go. Just keep moving forward—one step at a time.

You Are Here

Next Steps

- _____
- _____
- _____

Your Successful Future Is Here

_____

_____

A Final Word

Take a look back at all you've accomplished as you've worked your way through this book.

- You made important discoveries about yourself and the world of work.
- You explored a wide variety of career ideas found along this career pathway.
- You've experimented with three success strategies.

At this point, you may or may not be satisfied that you've got your future all figured out. Chances are you still aren't quite sure. Chances are even greater that things will change (maybe even more than once) before you put your big plans into action. After all, who knows what you'll discover as you get out there and experience the real world in new and interesting ways.

One thing is certain though: You are in better shape now than you were when you started reading this book. Why? Because you now have tools you can use to make well-informed career decisions—as you take your first steps toward your future career and throughout your life as you pursue new opportunities.

You've been wrestling with three big questions throughout this book.

- What do you know a lot about?
- What are you really good at doing?
- Where can you put that knowledge and those skills to work?

Rely on these questions to point you toward new opportunities as you move along your career path. Adjust them to reflect your constantly evolving experience and expertise, of course. And, whenever you find yourself in need of a career compass, simply revisit those questions again.

Then update that knowledge, hone those skills, and look for an employer who is willing to pay you to do what you really want to do!

With all this said and done, there's just one more question to ask: What *are* you going to do when you graduate?

Appendix

CAREER IDEAS FOR TEENS SERIES

Find out more about the world of work in any of these *Career Ideas for Teens* titles:

- *Agriculture, Food, and Natural Resources*
- *Architecture and Construction*
- *Arts and Communications*
- *Business, Management, and Administration*
- *Education and Training*
- *Finance*
- *Government and Public Service*
- *Health Science*
- *Hospitality and Tourism*
- *Human Services*
- *Information Technology*
- *Law and Public Safety*
- *Manufacturing*
- *Marketing*
- *Science, Technology, Engineering, and Math*
- *Transportation, Distribution, and Logistics*

VIRTUAL SUPPORT TEAM

As you continue your quest to determine just what it is you want to do with your life, you'll find that you are not alone. There are many people and organizations who want to help you succeed. Here are two words of advice: let them! Take advantage of all the wonderful resources so readily available to you.

The first place to start is your school's guidance center. There you will probably find a variety of free resources, which include information about careers, colleges, and other types of training opportunities; details about interesting events, job shadowing activities, and internship options; and access to useful career assessment tools.

In addition, there's a world of information just a mouse click away—use it! The following Internet resources provide all kinds of information and ideas that can help you find your future.

MAKE AN INFORMED CHOICE

Following are three especially useful career Web sites. Be sure to bookmark and visit them often as you consider various career options.

America's Career InfoNet

http://www.acinet.org

Quite possibly the most comprehensive source of career exploration anywhere, this U.S. Department of Labor Web site includes all kinds of current information about wages, market conditions, employers, and employment trends. Make sure to visit the site's career video library where you'll find links to more than 450 videos featuring real people doing real jobs.

Careers & Colleges

http://www.careersandcolleges.com

Here you'll find useful information about college, majors, scholarships, and other training options.

Career OneStop–Students and Career Advisors

http://www.careeronestop.org/studentsandcareeradvisors/
studentsandcareeradvisors.aspx

This Web site is brought to you compliments of the U.S. Department of Labor, Employment and Training Administration, and is designed especially for students like you. Here you'll find information on occupations and industries, internships, schools, and more.

GET A JOB

Whether you're curious about the kinds of jobs currently in big demand or you're actually looking for a job, the following Web sites are a great place to do some virtual job-hunting:

America's Job Bank

http://www.ajb.org

Another example of your (or, more accurately, your parents') tax dollars at work, this well-organized Web site is sponsored by the U.S. Department of Labor. Job seekers can post résumés and use the site's search engines to search through more than a million job listings by location or by job type.

Monster.com
http://www.monster.com

One of the Internet's most widely used employment Web sites, this is where you can search for specific types of jobs in specific parts of the country, network with millions of people, and find useful career advice.

Career Builder
http://www.careerbuilder.com

Another mega-career Web site where you can find out more about what employers are looking for in employees and get a better idea about in-demand professions.

EXPLORE BY CAREER PATHWAY

An especially effective way to explore career options is to look at careers associated with a personal interest or fascination with a certain type of industry. The following Web sites help you narrow down your options in a focused way:

All Career Clusters
Careership
http://mappingyourfuture.org/planyourcareer/careership

Find careers related to any of the 16 career clusters by clicking on the "Review Careers by Cluster" icon.

Agriculture, Food, and Natural Resources
Agrow Knowledge
http://www.agrowknow.org/

Grow your knowledge about this career pathway at the National Resource Center for Agriscience and Technology Education Web site.

Architecture and Construction

Construct My Future

http://www.constructmyfuture.com

    With more than $600 billion annually devoted to new construction projects, about 6 million Americans build careers in this industry. This Web site, sponsored by the Association of Equipment Distributors Foundation, Association of Equipment Manufacturers, Associated General Contractors, introduces an interesting array of construction-related professions.

Make It Happen

http://www.buildingcareers.org

    Another informative construction-related Web site—this one sponsored by the Home Builders Institute.

Arts and Communications

My Arts Career

http://www.myartscareer.org

    Find out how to put your artistic talents to work at this Web site sponsored by the Center for Arts Education.

Business, Management, and Administration

Careers in Business

http://www.careers-in-business.com

    Find links to help you get down to the business of finding a career in business.

Education and Training

Careership

http://mappingyourfuture.org/planyourcareer/careership

    Find careers related to education, training, and library by clicking on the "Review Careers by Cluster" icon.

Finance

Careers in Finance

http://www.careers-in-finance.com/

    Find a wide variety of links related to careers in finance.

Government and Public Service
Public Service Careers
http://www.publicservicecareers.org

This authoritative Web site is cohosted by the National Association of Schools of Public Affairs and Administration and the American Society for Public Administration.

Health Science
Campaign for Nursing Future
http://campaignfornursing.com/nursing-careers

Here's where to find information on nursing careers from A–Z.

Discover Nursing
http://www.discovernursing.com

More helpful information on nursing opportunities for men, women, minorities, and people with disabilities brought to you by Johnson & Johnson.

Explore Health Careers
http://explorehealthcareers.org/en/Field/1/Allied_Health
    _Professions

Find out about nearly 200 allied health careers at this informative Web site.

Hospitality and Tourism
O*Net Hospitality and Tourism Career Cluster
http://online.onetcenter.org/find/career?c=9

Visit this useful Web site to see career profiles about a wide variety of hospitality and tourism positions.

Human Services
Health and Human Services
http://www.hhs.gov

Explore federal health and human services opportunities associated with the U.S. Department of Health and Human Services.

Information Technology

Pathways to Technology

http://www.pathwaystotechnology.org/index.html

Find ideas and information about careers associated with all kinds of state-of-the-art and emerging technologies.

Law and Public Safety

National Partnership for Careers in Law, Public Safety, Corrections and Security

http://www.ncn-npcpss.com/

Initially established with funding from the U.S. Department of Justice, this organization partners with local and federal public safety agencies, secondary and postsecondary education institutions, and an array of professional and educational associations to build and support career-development resources.

Manufacturing

Dream It, Do It

http://www.dreamit-doit.com/index.php

The National Association of Manufacturers and the Manufacturing Institute created the Dream It, Do It campaign to educate young adults and their parents, educators, communities, and policy-makers about manufacturing's future and its careers. This Web site introduces high-demand 21st-century manufacturing professions many will find surprising and worthy of serious consideration.

Cool Stuff Being Made

http://www.youtube.com/user/NAMvideo

See for yourself how some of your favorite products are made compliments of the National Association of Manufacturers.

Manufacturing Is Cool

http://www.manufacturingiscool.com

Get a behind-the-scenes look at how some of your favorite products are manufactured at this Society of Manufacturing Engineers Web site.

Marketing
Take Another Look

http://www.careers-in-marketing.com/

Here's where you'll find links to all kinds of information about opportunities in marketing.

Science, Technology, Engineering, and Math (STEM)
Project Lead the Way

http://www.pltw.org

This organization exists to prepare students to be innovative, productive leaders in STEM professions.

Transportation, Distribution, and Logistics
Garrett A. Morgan Technology and Transportation Futures Program for Ninth through Twelfth Grade

http://www.fhwa.dot.gov/education/9-12home.htm

Get moving to find links to all kinds of interesting transportation career resources.

Index

Page numbers in **bold** indicate major treatment of a topic.